Stolen Thunder

American University Studies

Series XV
Communications
Vol. 4

PETER LANG
New York • Washington, DC/Baltimore • San Francisco
Bern • Frankfurt am Main • Berlin • Vienna • Paris

Lisa St. Clair Harvey

Stolen Thunder

The Cultural Roots of Political Communication

PETER LANG
New York • Washington, DC/Baltimore • San Francisco
Bern • Frankfurt am Main • Berlin • Vienna • Paris

Library of Congress Cataloging-in-Publication Data

Harvey, Lisa St. Clair.
 Stolen thunder: the cultural roots of political communication / Lisa
St. Clair Harvey.
  p.   cm. — (American university studies, Series XV,
Communications; vol. 4)
 Includes bibliographical references
  1. Presidents—United States—Election. 2. Presidents—United States—
Election—1988. 3. Television in politics—United States. 4. Mass
media—Political aspects—United States. 5. Public opinion—United
States. I. Title. II. Series: American university studies. Series XV.
Communications; v. 4.
 JK524.H37   1994   324.973′0927—dc20   93-30456
 ISBN 0-8204-2339-4   CIP
 ISSN 0740-5111

Die Deutsche Bibliothek-CIP-Einheitsaufnahme

Harvey, Lisa St. Clair:
Stolen thunder: the cultural roots of political communication / Lisa St. Clair
Harvey. - New York; San Francisco; Bern; Baltimore; Frankfurt am Main;
Berlin; Wien; Paris: Lang, 1994
 (American university studies: Ser. 15, Communications; Vol. 4)
 ISBN 0-8204-2339-4
NE: American university studies / 15

Photo on the back cover is by Diane L. Borden.

The paper in this book meets the guidelines for permanence and durability of
the Committee on Production Guidelines for Book Longevity of the
Council on Library Resources.

© Peter Lang Publishing, Inc., New York 1994

Printed in the United States of America.

This work is dedicated to the memory of my father, Thomas Michael Harvey, who taught me that there could be truth as well as honor in public life, and to Dr. Diane L. Borden, for her support, companionship, steadfast affection and immense personal integrity.

Acknowledgements

The list could go on forever, but in particular I would like to thank Dr. Roger Simpson, for his intellectual guidance and personal support, as well as Drs. Simon Ottenberg, Richard Kielbowitz, W. Lance Bennett, Ed Bassett, Mary Whitlock-Blundell, and Kurt and Gladys Lang, all at the University of Washington, and Dr. Ella Taylor, formerly associated with that institution. Cohorts and classmates Nancy Rivenburgh, Bonnie Duncan, Carolyn Byerly, Patty Mullady, Mike Hindmarsh, Elisa Elder, Jiande Chen, and Diane Borden also kept me sane, kept me going, kept me awake, and kept me at the computer during this process, for which I am grateful as well as indebted. Special thanks go to Pat Dombrowski, for her cheerful and timely "bubble-ups" and priceless common sense; to Pat Dinning, who aided immeasurably in the first version of this work; and to all the good folks at Peter Lang Publishing, for their patience and good humor. In Washington, I am especially appreciative of Robin and Dana Netherton—especially Robin, who pulled me out of yet another pickle at a time when it counted most; my pal Sally Santen; and the staff and faculty—especially my supervisors, Jerry Manheim and Joan Thiel—at the George Washington University for their forebearance and understanding during a particularly rugged set of publishing deadlines. My deep personal thanks go to the entire Sterling clan—Chris, Ellen, Jennifer, and Robin—who so enriched both the rewrite process and the colorful emotional space within which it was located, and of course, to my own tribe, my mother Eleanor Harvey and my two sisters, Daphne and Teal, for all that I put them and their respective broods through during this protracted period of author angst. And, finally, I must reiterate my enduring appreciation of Peg England, a Nantucket Island friend of thirty years, whose encouragement and acceptance of a little girl's bubbling curiosity helped to nurture the intellectual impetus behind a lifetime of study and scholarly thought. To you all, I am deeply indebted, in a way that connects, rather than constrains, the spirit and the soul. Many thanks, and much love.

Table of Contents

List of Tables

Chapter I

Myth, Ritual, and National Psyche

Plato, of all people, was worried about, of all things, democracy. In his "Address to Gorgias," he outlined the many reasons why he felt that the general public was unfit to be the primary author of government (Plato 1928–61). Among his concerns was the fear that the electorate tended to make voting decisions based on emotion rather than on reason. Easy prey to demagogues and to charlatans, according to Plato, the public could be all-too-easily swayed by smooth rhetoric, empty phrases, and psychic, if not actual, bribery. The celebrated philosopher felt that "educated, upper-class people" (in Plato's restrictive political cosmology, educated, upper-class men) were likely to be better informed than the undifferentiated public about matters of common social concern. Therefore, they were the appropriate leaders in a self-governing community. The educated elite would be far less susceptible to demagoguery, and far more concerned with the long-term welfare of the entire community, than would be the fractious, self-absorbed "rabble," so the argument went, while the landed gentry would be invested—literally as well as symbolically—in actions that would best ensure the community's continued prosperity (Simpson 1987). In light of this deeply elitist attitude, it is, at first glance, somewhat astonishing that Plato enjoys consistent inclusion in the stable of classic philosophers on whom the intellectual foundations of the American version of democracy are usually presumed to rest.

The debate over who is best suited to govern, the common people or the educated elite, did not end with Plato, nor with the many spiritual heirs to representative democracy. Over and over again, the issue floats to the surface of history, presenting a series of awkward problems for the political leaders and the policy-makers of those eras in which it arises. From the halls of the Athenian Senate to the Rotunda of the United States Capitol, no one has yet has been able to find an easy way to settle this basic dilemma in self-governance. Many have tried, and many have failed ... or have, at best, enjoyed mixed results. Among these uncertain victors may be included the authors of those singular American governing documents, the Constitution and the Bill of Rights, who did not solve the problem, but who succeeded in spreading the responsibility for addressing it among three branches of government, presumably as a strategy for counterbalancing the undisciplined voice of public opinion.

1

The role played by public opinion in the contemporary American political arena remains difficult to understand. The first challenge, of course, is understanding exactly what is meant by the term "public opinion" itself. As many academic definitions exist for the phrase "public opinion" as there are scholars to hold them. Emerging from all of them is the central idea that public opinion is in some way an expression of the public will, although Kurt and Gladys Lang, among others, are quick to note that there are many "publics" in America, each of which may conceivably cling to its own unique collective "will." Further complicating the situation is the realization that public will is also, as the Langs put it, "unstable ... in flux ... and less than unanimous" (Lang and Lang 1983, 10–12).

Perhaps this is one viable definition of public will: The expression of a significant—although not necessarily dominant—sector of the population's attitudes, thoughts, and conclusions regarding people, affairs, or events of public importance, at any given time. The implicit distinction between *majority* opinion and *dominant* opinion is important, since control of the public stage—of the type available through exploitation of the broadcast media, for example—might give groups the appearance of majority when, in fact, they may not actually enjoy such privilege.

Determining just what contribution public opinion makes to the American political process is the first challenge. Figuring out whether or not that role is appropriate, by the standards and the spirit of Jefferson, Madison, and other Constitutional architects, is another matter. Further muddying the waters is the twentieth-century intrusion of the electronic media into the election environment. The campaign trail has become one large, perpetual "media event," with the ubiquitous presence of the television camera dictating to a considerable extent the tone, the style, and, some would claim, the substance of the candidates' courtship of the American voting public. How can we—voters, candidates, media players, and critics of the mass media alike—even begin to make sense of the orchestrated chaos which has come to characterize the U.S. political landscape?

One place to begin is by scrutinizing the fundamental questions used to frame the issue itself. Re-examining the reasons why Americans hold national elections might shed some light on the way in which they are conducted. This book explores the idea that the social function of the American presidential election process itself has been changed by the intervention of the mass media—most dramatically, by television. Although the manifest function of a presidential election is to select a new national leader, several of the latent functions involved in the election event may have overshadowed this task. In other words, the contemporary act of holding an election may have travelled some distance from the original function of elections. In anthropological terms, the manifest (surface) and the latent (hidden) aspects of election-holding as a social activity may differ significantly. Particularly interesting is the notion that, through the unique qualities of television, presidential elections in particular may have evolved into a public ritual whose primary social function is to periodically provide a public forum for the discussion, selection, and subsequent re-validation of politically privileged cultural myth. Picking someone to actually run the United States may be an after-thought to using the election as a place to hammer out what the United States "stands for" in ideological terms.

Shifting the analytical focus to address the issue from this angle requires that scholars expand their vision of the election phenomenon itself, looking at what happens between elections as well as what happens during an election, try-ing to establish patterns of interaction between the anthropological uses of politi-cal communication and other dimensions of the social arena. Critics and analysts alike have pointed out that the 1988 contest was perhaps more mass-mediated than any previous presidential election. Democratic candidate Michael Dukakis lost his bid for the presidency not through any lack of personal competence, but rather through the feeble, fumbling impression he left flickering on millions of American television sets—and in the minds of millions of American voters—by his poor performance in the second presidential debate. The media, ironically, recognized this. Writers in the *New York Times*, the *Washington Post*, and the *New Yorker* magazine all took swipes at the gritty trivia around which campaign "issues" were built. George Bush himself admitted to some mixed feelings about the guerrilla tactics to which he resorted as part of the Republican campaign strategy (Wills 1988, 70).

But although the consensus seems to be clear that the Bush-Dukakis race was an intensely mass-mediated phenomenon, no one seems to be certain how this situation really affected the American voter, nor to have a clear focus on what historical trends, if any, may have led to this situation. The topic is huge, but not insurmountable. The place to begin unraveling this behemoth puzzle is with an understanding of the fashion in which complicated political issues relate to the generation and perpetuation of cultural myth, and by exploring the relationship between cultural systems and social thought.

Media involvement in the election process can be divided into three dis-tinct categories. First, there is the "campaign coverage," the purportedly "objective" reporting of information about the candidates and their relative progress in pursuit of voter support. Included in this coverage is material about how the various candidates are "doing" in the fickle affections of the electorate. This is usually presented in the form of public opinion polls, although less for-mal versions, such as "person on the street" interviews, are also included. Statements made directly to the media by the candidates themselves, or by sur-rogates for the candidates, such as wives, children, and increasingly husbands, form a second category of media participation. And, finally, media-generated material about the media's own involvement with the election, such as televised analyses of televised political debates or interview programs in which one "television personality" probes another's views on campaign happenings, supplies yet a third bundle of mass-mediated information about "democracy in action."

In order to understand the election process, one must first comprehend the influence of all of the "message packages" on the role played by public opinion in shaping political landscapes long before the arrival of election day. American internal political struggles are complex and somewhat painful phenomena, and their final outcome determines the leadership of one of the world's most powerful nations for a period of at least four years. We Americans cannot find real meaning in the effects of our electoral procedures unless we fully grasp the nature and character of the many contributing causes, and their strength or weakness relative to one another.

Since the United States is structured as a representative democracy, foremost among these "contributing causes" must be listed the power of the public will. But we can't really get traction on the role of public opinion unless we also develop a clear understanding of the role of the media. Down and around and around it goes—a seemingly endless chain of cause and effect and countereffect. So directly have the media been implicated in the molding of public thought that, to a significant degree, the two entities have become functionally inseparable. In fact, a sense of culture itself as an extended system of communication has come a long way since its introduction in the 1960s. And, since that time, many fine studies of the relationship between the mass media and the formation of American political thought have been conducted—including numerous studies regarding the effect of televised debates between candidates. But as Joseph Klapper (1960) has suggested, claiming a direct and causal link between the formation of public opinion and public exposure to the mass media is dangerously misleading.

Klapper maintains that communication efforts reinforce old social attitudes more often than they create new ones, a notion which is echoed by Elihu Katz's conclusion (Lang and Lang 1983, 6) that "Effects ... depend not on what the mass media do to people so much as on what people do with the mass media." This, and similar observations by the Langs, support the idea that the evolution of public will does not occur solely within the temporal confines of the election process. That is to say, events which unfold during the campaign itself are the logical—and to some degree, the inevitable—descendants of political attitudes and social emotions which have been percolating in the cultural soup long before the election process began. Our choice of presidents is determined not so much by what happens during the campaign, as by what happens between campaigns. This, in turn, implies that the outcomes of our national elections are not the result of a brief, vicious political spasm which occurs once every four years, but rather are the product of long-term social trends and slow, weighty shifts in public thought. And this introduces the question of what actually happens to cultural myth once it enters the political climate.

"Myth," in general, can be defined as a culturally sustained and generated image or narrative that has as its sub-text a socially important moral, message, or lesson. Although this is a fairly loose definition, its elasticity is consistent with the fluid but persistent character of myth itself, both *in situ* within cultures and as it wriggles around, decontextualized, under the probing finger of social science research. Indeed, one of the main attributes of myth, as Roland Barthes (1972) describes it, is that myth is almost impossible to "pin down." It consists, claims Barthes, of culturally specific stories about universal truths. It is this intensely interpretative character of myth, relative to the society from which it was produced, which so fascinated Barthes, and which is also so intriguing in terms of its political dimensions.

Ritual, as Barthes (1972) and others describe it, is the operationalization of myth within specific and culturally appropriate times and places. Ritual is a series of actions or enactments which reinforce the "lessons" and the socially defined "realities" encoded in mythic stories. Without myth, ritual would be empty and useless, for it is only through belief in the myths of any given culture that the rituals of that culture can find social nerves to touch and chambers of the collective heart in which to resonate.

Clearly, this function of myth is closely tied to the notion of hegemony—the idea that ambitious groups within a pluralistic society can achieve domination over others by using myth to explain away institutionalized social inequities and to cloak continuing economic disadvantaging. Those who control the means of manufacturing the images of hegemonic culture also exert a disproportionate influence on that society's political sensibilities and subsequent political character. Understanding the specific mechanics of how this occurs is a goal of the first importance.

Much has been written on the evolution of public thought in the political sphere, but it is important to reconcile this work with other aspects of the body politic—in other words, to understand the cultural implications of the mass media/government liaison as way of comprehending the cultural roots of political sensibilities.

Bennett (1980), for example, raises an important but puzzling point:

> The persistence of simple and redundant political solutions is remarkable in light of their typical failure to resolve the social and economic problems they address. In order for issues to fit so readily into familiar but dubious symbolic formats there must be a special logic that organizes the political communications among elites and the general public. (166)

He goes on to suggest that it is cultural myth which provides the conceptual "logic" which underlies these persistently ineffectual methods of political problem-solving. "Myths are used as models," writes Bennett, "for applying the values and beliefs from which public opinion emerges" (168).

Bennett's conclusion is that:

> ... The idea that policies (and other political outcomes) are important
> variables in larger communication processes that reinforce key po-
> litical myths explains a number of curious features of American pol-
> itics. For example, this idea helps explain why policies need not be
> particularly effective in order to be popular. The fact that policies
> (and the social problems they address) are more likely to be evaluat-
> ed against prevailing myth than against rational empirical criteria
> also explains why the past failure of a policy is no guarantee that it
> will not be used again in the future. (173)

The maintenance of these mythic illusions, Bennett suggests, may be more
important to the maintenance of culture than the development of effective political solutions that challenge the prevailing systems of myth. This hypothesis
assumes a particularly sinister tone when placed within the context of a representative system of self-government. If Bennett's perception is accurate, then our
election events occur on at least two separate levels of cultural function—two
levels which may be characterized to a large extent by their competing conceptual agenda. It is a "heart vs. head" type of dilemma. Candidates who require us
to recognize that belief does not always correspond to reality may be effective as
administrators, but they are seldom popular as leaders. Unpopular candidates are,
by definition, un-electable, no matter how "realistic" they may be.

Traditionally, media scholars seeking to understand which candidates get
elected, and why, have focused on the political communication which their campaigns design and generate—or which their unsuccessful competition doesn't. But
what if all of this scholarship has been barking up the wrong campaign stump, as it
were, because presidential elections themselves have less to do with politics than
they have to do with culture? What if something else, something more, is happening every time Americans walk into a voting booth and push some candidate's buttons? What if elections have more to do with public debate over the nation's self-
image than with specific personnel changes in the Oval Office? If that is the case,
then perhaps the failings, the flounderings, the rather spectacular public atrophy
which some claim thwarts our continued attempts at self-government are due not to
how we hold elections, but rather to *why* we hold them.

We Americans may be using our elective processes to reassure ourselves
of the continuing validity of our core cultural myths, rather than to select effective world leaders. If that is indeed the case, that level of self-deception might be
as corrosive as it is confusing. We must recognize our social events for what
they truly are, or we run the risk of not recognizing where our cultural mechanism falls short. There is no point in calling a spade a spade, for example, when
in point of fact it gets used primarily as a hammer, and if one persists in calling

that particular tool a hammer long enough, then sooner or later society is saddled with a whole generation of young people who never realize that an entire range of tools exist, some of which give them the option to dig rather than to pound.

Clearly, if we want to understand the cultural dynamics which operate within our national political system, we must also comprehend the erratic internal "logic" regulating our national mythology. Furthermore, we must understand the working relationship between these two—a relationship which may be more of an arranged marriage than a true affair of the heart.

Getting at some of the nuts and bolts of how this relationship might operate is the driving idea behind this book. Since they happen on a grand scale—literally, a world stage—presidential politics provide a more rewarding lode to mine than do state or local elections. Conceptual as well as methodological reasons support this, since presidential elections are qualitatively different from anything else that happens in the United States. The stakes are higher, the players are "bigger," and the mechanisms employed to convert cultural raw materials into political ante show up more boldly. One particularly pertinent case in point is the 1988 American presidential election. But a few specialized terms must be introduced before focusing on this particular moment in American public life. Specifically, distinctions must be drawn among several different types of cultural myth—*long-term*, or sustaining myths of culture; *short-term*, or disposable myth; and *mythic images*.

Here are some examples of the differences among these concepts. A sustaining myth of culture can be thought of as a story, a story with a moral or a model or a cultural lesson embedded within its narrative structure. These lessons articulate the cultural values and social expectations which define the rules of order along which the host society is organized and within which its particular vision of the world is shaped. The now-mythic story of the doomed little fort named "The Alamo," for example, articulates the "American values" of rugged independence, extreme self-reliance, loyalty to like-minded peers, and heroic persistence despite overwhelming opposition.

A short-term, or disposable, myth is more specific in content, but less concrete in form. Its purpose is to trigger within its audience all of the individual emotions, group political reactions, and general social impressions contained within the longer version—within the sustaining cultural myth—but to harness these visceral feelings to a specific political goal. A good example of a disposable or short-term myth would be the concept of "Texas," which is a shorthand way of referencing the whole geo-historical complex behind the idea of the American male as a product of the American frontier. To continue the earlier illustration, "Texas" is the disposable myth version of the sustaining myth of the Alamo; the Alamo was located in Texas, for one thing, and the ill-fated battle for that unfortunate fort involved many famous frontiersmen from all over the West, whose stubborn, blazing defeat epitomized the "American" ideal of fighting injustice to the last living man.

Metaphorically speaking, the sustaining myth of the Alamo is a kind of film; the short-term myth of "Texas" is a snapshot, lifted out of that film, which captures in condensed form the point and the feeling of the longer story. A measure of the "disposability" of these short-term myths is the ease with which they are discarded once their job is done, or, conversely, the care with which they are maintained as they continue to perform their assigned political functions within related settings.

A mythic image is a specific, indexical fragment of either type of myth which has been, through intent or by accident, cut loose from its moorings within the narrative structure. Again, the importance of this is primarily political. Mythic images are disposable myths "on assignment," so to speak. They make concrete the salient bits and pieces of sustaining myth that float around in the cultural ether, unattached but nonetheless politically potent. To complete the Texas example, the successful short-term myth of George Bush as an all-American leader—a tough, self-reliant man molded in the tradition of the American frontier male—was well-sustained throughout the pre-election period by constant reference to Bush as a "Texas boy," despite the material fact that the then vice president was much more of a New England "preppie" than he was a Southwestern cowboy. But carefully tended lingering mythic images kept the idea of Bush as "Western guy" alive long after the election had been won, by resurrecting the short-term image periodically through homey social events and media performances, such as White House barbecues.

What happens to a mythic image once it's released into the political ozone? In a media-driven environment like the United States, it usually encounters other mythic images, with which it then struggles for primacy in the public mind. For example, the Democratic parry to Bush's tough-but-genial cowboy image was to put their candidate in a tank, in an effort to make a memorable visual statement about Dukakis's own affinity for things masculine and for military strength in the American tradition. For the Democrats, compounding the simple image problem was the strong political message with which it had been coupled: George Bush is a real American man and he'll keep our country strong. Michael Dukakis's more complicated stance on military strength, in which he advocated cutting back on nuclear armament and dumping altogether the "Star Wars" program so dear to the Reagan White House, put the Democrats in the position of having to develop their own short-term myth to make the rather complex point that Dukakis wasn't against a strong military, *per se*—he just wanted to spend the defense budget dollar differently than did George Bush. The tank was their answer. But they ran into a cultural problem here, because tanks don't have the same deep resonance in American cultural symbolism as does the Alamo. It's more difficult to explain what a tank stands for; it takes more work, and so the short-term myth which the Democrats developed failed, quickly and miserably, in part because their symbolism was too cumbersome and lacked instant cultural recognition, and in part because it just didn't mesh with the personal and visual attributes of the candidate to whom it was pinned.

Roland Barthes (1972) claims that myth is "de-politicized language," that it is language which so reifies the status quo that it appears to describe things which are universally believed to be true, even if they are not. If this is, indeed, the case with all myth, then disposable myth is reification of culture in a particularly virulent form. One may say that political myth is cultural myth that has forgotten its roots, but has sharpened its sense of ambition.

Stolen Thunder explores the idea that the most effective political messages have little to do with issues—or even with candidates—and everything to do with cultural story-telling. It explores the possibility that the most effective political messages are those which have one foot in culture and the other in collective anxiety, and it suggests that new and innovative research methods must be developed in order to probe more deeply this buried aspect of the national political psyche.

In particular, it examines the role of television in the formation, transmission, and occasional reconfiguration of sustaining cultural myth, and tests the proposition that short-term variations of these myths are developed for their political utility in the election setting. Employing a combination of textual analysis, survey data, content analysis, and inquiries probing the subjunctive mode of political culture to reconstruct the campaign mythology of both 1988 presidential candidates, and to chart the growing influence of media-generated myth throughout the symbolic context in which the formation of public attitudes occurs, the study does not seek to answer questions so much as it seeks to develop a set of cultural and political questions which might be worth asking, and a vision of the cultural scenario in which their impact is most likely to be felt.

The opening scene in that unfolding picture of the American cultural landscape is a surprising one. The first stop in charting tele-politics in the 20th century is to revisit the restless British colonies of the late 1700s, to see what specific bits and pieces of the European Enlightenment were used to buttress the American vision of self-government. And the next stop after that one, even more surprisingly, is the calamitous and chaotic "drug war" of the mid-1980s.

Chapter II

The Return of God's Anointed:
Mythic Imagery and Political Expediency
in the 1980s "War on Drugs"

The highly publicized "war on drugs" which figured so conspicuously in much of the 1988 pre-election campaign rhetoric provides a good example of the way in which cultural myths can be deliberately shaped into politically expedient social attitudes through the use of the mass media. Interestingly, this issue provoked much passionate reaction from the political perception survey respondents and from the advertisement panel analysts who participated in the research for this book, and whose responses will be discussed shortly.

During the campaign, both Bush and Dukakis positioned the need to "crack down" on the illegal use of narcotics as one of the most critical challenges facing the United States. Drug use, drug trafficking, and drug-related crimes were defined as America's "number-one social problem," more important than the country's financial woes or deteriorating race relations. This privileging of the drug issue over other, perhaps equally pressing social problems is vitally important in light of the role played by cultural myth in the political arena, because in the 1988 pre-election campaign rhetoric, the "war on drugs" became a symbolic setting for the trench warfare of democracy.

Advance groundwork for re-framing drug abuse as a national security issue began about halfway through the second Reagan Administration, when his First Lady embraced the issue as her personal mission. Although its usefulness as an addiction prevention device may be questionable, Nancy Reagan's "Just Say No" campaign did accomplish several politically strategic goals.

First, it rocketed the drug topic into the national limelight, thus targeting it for media attention and preparing the way for its eventual evolution into a campaign issue, two years down the road. Second, it made personal decisions regarding the use of illegal drugs a matter of ethical choice, predicated on the exercise of individual willpower rather than on chemical dependency. This was, in fact, a giant step backwards into an earlier, more puritanical era, when "weakness"—the inability to say "no"—was the conceptual equivalent of "sin." The most interesting thing about the strategy was that it worked, despite efforts by Alcoholics Anonymous and other spearheads of the "clean and sober" movement to couch substance abuse in medical rather than in moral terms. Mrs. Reagan's "willpower is enough" attitude simply did not jibe with scientific conceptualizations of chemical addiction as a disease; it made as much medical sense as would slogans like "Just Say No to Diabetes" or "Just Say No to Glaucoma." But despite its flawed logic, the "Zero Tolerance" campaign caught hold—and caught the eye of the national press. Toward the end of 1988, as the Reagan Administration geared down, the "war on drugs" heated up, until by the time the presidential primaries had arrived, it was the kind of red-hot political issue that could help make or break a candidacy.

Serious strategy development for the 1988 presidential race began for the Republican team on Memorial Day, at the vice president's family retreat in Kennebunkport. Press folklore has it that, just prior to this marathon brainstorming session, former Reagan White House speechwriter Peggy Noonan happened to tune in to a radio spot that the Bush people had produced for the New Hampshire primaries. Horrified at what she heard, she rallied back to the Republican hearth, where her considerable talents were linked to extensive and professionally conducted focus group research used to identify issues most likely to evoke impassioned reactions from the American voting public. Drug abuse, and all of the malevolent social baggage which accompanies it, was among the top contenders (Stengel and others 1988, 48–56).

At Kennebunkport, an impressive clutch of Republican strategists had assembled to diagram their candidate's political war plans. John Sununu, then the state chairman for Bush in New Hampshire, "media handler" Roger Ailes, and Republican Party luminaries Lee Atwater, Nicholas Brady, Richard Darman, among others, developed a battery of powerful strategies for turning social issues into political missiles pointed at Dukakis. Although the vice president was reportedly uncomfortable with the negative dimension of their plan, he nonetheless agreed to it in the end.

This was in May. In August, the Dukakis camp was just beginning to identify issues to be embraced as themes for their own campaign—not realizing, apparently, that the four months which elapsed between May and August eroded any hope they may have had of defining the grounds of political battle on their own terms. Their delay cost them a critical edge in setting the agenda of the presidential contest—an edge that the Bush people were quick to scoop up. It wasn't until after the first presidential debate in the fall that Dukakis and his staff finally agreed on the nature and the content of their arsenal. At that point, they, also, included drugs on the list of subjects over which to grapple with Vice President Bush.

The two general strategies, however, were somewhat different. In a bid to link domestic drug abuse with unsavory foreign elements and with the abuse of power by American officials, the Dukakis people focused much of their effort on forcing the "Iran-contra" issue into the public eye. But their attempts to stigmatize Bush as a back room drug thug failed, perhaps, in part, because, having identified a sordid goal, they nonetheless insisted on pursuing it high-handedly. Another major factor in the Democratic failure was the simple fact that the Bush people refused to be frightened by the Dukakis attack.

By the time of the second presidential debate, Bush had managed to steal the wind from "Iran-contra" with his Willie Horton and Boston Harbor counter-attacks, and had gutted the Iranian event's political liability by re-framing it as just another instance of what he called "Democratic whining." Just before the second debate, Bush's pugnacious media adviser, Roger Ailes, told him "If he (Dukakis) brings up Iran-contra, just walk over there and deck him" (Stengel and others 1988, 56). It didn't happen exactly that way, but close—when Dukakis brought up the uncomfortably cozy association between the Vice President and Panamanian drug lord Manuel Noriega, Bush's exaggerated contempt for the issue, as well as for the accusation, defused its political volatility once and for all.

But the issue of drugs was still very much present on the symbolic scene, separate and distinct from Central American hijinks. Both Bush and Dukakis continued to milk the drug issue for all it was worth, using it as a vehicle through which to convey their contrasting attitudes about a number of different social problems—such as whether to assign the death penalty for drug lords and if mandatory drug testing violated Constitutional rights to privacy. Margaret Carlson, writing in the November 21, 1988, issue of *Time*, noted that:

> A visitor from another planet would surely have thought that the presidential race was about prison furloughs, the death penalty for drug kingpins, mandatory pledge of allegiance, and Dan Quayle's I.Q.... Still, the noise generated by these contentious non-issues may have kept voters from focusing on Michael Dukakis' talking points.... Among the 21% (of voters) who considered drugs to be the most important campaign issue, the vote split evenly, despite Dukakis' efforts to tie Bush to the "drug-running Panamanian dictator Manuel Noriega." (37)

To understand how the two campaigns capitalized on drugs from a cultural as well as a political perspective, it's necessary to first examine the peculiarly American socio-historical context contributes to the emotional charge that drug abuse seems to carry for the American public.

The point of this exploration is not to determine whether so much alarm—and so much attention—is justified by the narcotics situation. Rather, it is to discuss the degree to which the political imagery about the war on drugs, generated by and revolving around the campaign promises of the 1988 presidential candidates, may differ from public perception of the same problem—and, if so, why that may be. Along the same lines, it's crucial to investigate the possibility that a social issue laden with deep-rooted cultural myth can be strategically relocated to yield short-term political gain, because if this can happen with drugs, it can happen with other, equally salient topics, like health care, reproductive rights, gun control, and Acquired Immune Deficiency Syndrome (AIDS) research. By chasing down what happened with the drug issue in the 1988 election, we can focus on a single issue and follow its transformation from a sustaining myth of culture to a disposable political myth.

The 1988 voters may have been, to some degree, aware of the differences between what the candidates told them were America's "big problems" and what they, themselves, identified as critically problematic. Data collected by means of both a political perception survey (PPS) and an advertising panel analysis, conducted during the 1988 election year cycle, indicate a conflicted image of drugs and their malevolent place in the public life of the late 1980s. In the PPS, for example, respondents were asked to identify issues they remembered as being the three main topics during the campaign. Later, on the same instrument, they were asked to explain which single problem they, themselves, would solve if they were given unlimited executive power.

Taxes, the federal deficit, and defense spending issues were cited as the three main issues of the campaign, garnering (from a total of 283 cases) 114 votes, 106 votes, and 84 votes, respectively. Addressing drugs and drug-related crime ranked only eighth (27 votes) on a field of 42 possible items.

Similarly, drug abuse fell behind the deficit (56 votes) and the homeless issue (27 votes), ranking third on the list of America's most pressing problems by garnering a mere 22 votes from a possible 283, as a problem which the respondents said they'd try to solve if they were the President.

It's possible that people might not have devoted too much new attention to drugs as a campaign issue because they had already made up their collective mind that drugs were more of a problem than traditional enemies—communism, pollution, and domestic violence, for example—as a major threat to the country's moral and social well-being. This, in turn, implies a qualitative change in the public's perception of both drugs and "enemies." Such a massive shift in public opinion, as Kurt and Gladys Lang (1983) have suggested in other arenas, had to begin before the campaign, laying the groundwork for subsequent symbolic events of the type displayed during the summer and fall of 1988.

Efforts on the part of the candidates to squeeze significant pre-election mileage out of the drug issue may, at first, have met with limited success, since relatively few people clung to the image of drugs as the salient campaign issue. But as the election year progressed, drugs quickly became a political axe to grind—and to brandish at one's political opponents.

One important but often overlooked result of setting up drugs as the new national villain is the opportunity it afforded both candidates to display what they considered to be "appropriate" villain-fighting attributes. Every drama needs a stage; every white knight needs a dragon; every successful re-enactment of any hero myth, in short, needs an irredeemably evil figure against whom epic struggle can be waged.

In 1988, softening relations between the United States and what is now the former Soviet Union had, to some extent, disqualified the Russians for this uncertain honor as national villain. Public outrage at the so-called "Japanese invasion" of prime American investment real estate smacked of residual racism from the Second World War; trying to pin the unadulterated blame for dwindling economic prosperity on any single public institution seemed as futile as much as it was culturally unjust. In this context, who was left to blame for America's woes? In the logic of the 1988 presidential campaign, the answer was: Drugs.

And blaming drugs, pinning on them the prime responsibility for so many of the country's social and economic failings, then provided a superb backdrop against which candidates—and presidents—could stand tall and strong in the public vision. It gave them, and the public, something good to hate. Why? Because a drug war is a safe crusade, since no single ethnic or racial group is overtly scapegoated; it provides a forum for politically correct hate. And hate has always been a force to contend with in national politics, if for no other reason than because it hammers fractured cultures together in resistance to a common enemy. Hate provides a reason to unite, just as surely and just as effectively as does greed, or disaster, or, sometimes, hope. Declaring a national and united "war on drugs" permitted the 1988 presidential candidates to re-enact many of the most cherished sustaining myths of American culture, which would have no longer worked in the national consciousness had they been deployed against racial or ethnic minorities or against more "traditional" external villains, like the Russians.

But against the indisputably evil influence of illegal drug use, the candidates could, in all good faith, demonstrate the types of leadership qualities which invoke central myths regarding warrior-kings. They could be "tough," "decisive," and "unrelenting," without having to worry about stepping on any Affirmative Action-protected toes. In short, the most important political mileage gained by the 1988 candidates by adopting the war on drugs as a major campaign issue worked in far more subtle and complex ways than as a simple frontal assault on coveted moral territory. It achieved a stolen march, a guerrilla movement by which each candidate sought to out-flank the other, strutting his own leadership style vis a vis the drug issue. Here's how those styles contrasted in ways that proved to be consistent with the overall leadership model that each candidate tried to peddle to the voting public.

Dukakis tried to be "intelligent" about the drug problem. Bush sold himself as "tough." Although exploratory, the research presented here suggests that, in each case, each man used the drug issue as a platform from which to display those personal traits he felt were most characteristic of himself and also most appealing to the American voting public as "presidential" attributes. Drugs, put simply, served as a magnifying lens through which the distinctive leadership mythology of each 1988 presidential finalist could be beamed, in enlarged, exaggerated fashion, at the American people.

None of this, of course, could have happened in a vacuum. Deep in the sustaining mythology of American culture, moral and dramatic elements making possible the strategic re-alignment of drugs and enemies had to be found, extracted, and massaged into shape for the 1988 campaign. To some degree, the candidates did nothing more sinister than to build on what must have already been there. But it is absolutely crucial that those who seek to understand the role of the media in shaping both the symbolic environment itself and the political agenda of symbolic events take into account the cultural, historical, and economic antecedents to political action. Without so deep and layered an awareness, political analysis remains dangerously one-dimensional and perilously isolated from its total meaning within a true cultural context. What this means is that contemporary analysts of political communication must look at the role of the symbolic environment in shaping political thought. And that story, for the 1988 election, began much further back in the human record than American history, *per se*, extends. The story begins with the externalization of "evil" onto concrete, physical, people and things. It begins with the demonization of cultural difference.

Symbolic environment and public thought

In the distant days before the fifteenth century, when human politics and divine intervention were inextricably and unabashedly linked, political symbols served as conceptual boundary-markers, staking out the coincidental spheres of influence enjoyed by various social institutions. Since the governing bodies of that day were in collusion with each other just as often as they were in competition for control of earthly affairs, clear distinctions between religious and secular symbology were unnecessary—were, in fact, sometimes awkward, as when the failure of the Fifth Crusade focused public attention on the blatant financial grasping of the Church at the expense of national unity in the secular realm. Except in moments of carefully orchestrated theological crisis, such as the Crusades or the Inquisition, God and the Crown had an almost equal claim on the soul—and the pocketbook—of the average person, and the same general set of symbols could be used to excite religious enthusiasm as to cultivate political loyalty among the general population.

But the events of the 15th and 16th centuries altered forever human ideas about the role of Providence in the governing process. Martin Luther's raid on the moral larders of the Church shifted the burden of ethical responsibility for personal action from the institution—in this case, the Church—to the individual. Luther's assertion that each man should be his own priest was an early step toward individual moral autonomy, for the male half of the population, at least. This radical notion enjoyed additional propulsion from the political developments accompanying the Protestant Reformation and the social upheavals in France and the fledgling United States. As historian Roger Simpson (1987) notes, once the concept of the "social contract" superseded the notion of "divine right to governance" as the dominant paradigm in political thought, the nature and the role of the political symbol, *per se*, had to change accordingly.

Enlightenment-era writers, developing their concept of the "rational man" as the basic unit of self-government, assumed that the emotional intensity of religious symbolism would lose much of its appeal when confronted by educated free thinkers in the political sphere. This idea underlies most if not all of the American governing documents. The Constitution, in particular, relies for its operational viability on the premise that given all the necessary information and an open forum in which to debate all the appropriate options, human beings will eventually base their political decisions and will design their social arrangements in a manner which brings the most benefit to the greatest number of people.

This assumption soon proved to be more hopeful than realistic, since without much apparent effort, the visceral appeal traditionally associated with religious fervor migrated to the political arena. Rising nationalistic tendencies among 16th century European states, and the startling rejection of the "Mother Country" by the American colonies during the late 1700s, ensured that zealotry would continue in one form or another. As Harold Lasswell (1966) notes in "Nations and Classes: The Symbols of Identification":

> The modern phenomenon of nationalism represents a complicated synthesis of religious, cultural, state, democratic, and allied patterns. Once partly integrated around a particular symbol, each new configuration diffused as a cultural complex, eliciting fresh acts of identification from some, and provoking decisive acts of rejection from others.... For better or for worse, we are embedded in historical configurations which are characterized by the existence of a large number of comprehensive symbols in the name of which people die or kill. (35)

Lasswell's perception of what constitutes a "symbol" is remarkably elastic, encompassing as it does anything which stands for, implies, infers, or imputes something else. What is critical here is the understanding that the importance of symbolic perceptions increases in proportion to the distance at which the symbolized object is seen. These cultural symbols, distantly linked to the realities they index, play an enormously important role in what Gaye Tuchman (1978) and others have called the "social construction of reality," the collection of essentially ideological perceptions, assumptions, and values upon which political sensibilities are ultimately based.

Part of the problem is size. Democracy works best in small, intimate communities, characterized by a high degree of face-to-face interaction. The central dilemma in any large, industrialized society is how to get accurate information about its constituent groups distributed to all of the groups which share psychic

space, in a way which lets the leadership groups—the elites, elected or otherwise—make decisions of benefit to all. As Walter Lippmann (1966) noted in his
seminal work on stereotyping, one natural reaction to information overload is to
fall back on surface imagery as a means of navigating a crowded, noisy, and
increasingly confusing world:

> For the most part, we do not see, and then define, we define first and
> then see. In the great blooming, buzzing confusion of the outer
> world, we pick out what the culture has already defined for us, and
> we tend to perceive that which we have picked out in the form of ste-
> reotypes. (68)

In the situation which Lippmann describes, individual perceptions of people and events—and of political situations—are filtered through a lens of consen-
sually based, culturally generated social definitions. There are some good reasons
why this happens, maintains Lippmann:

> There is economy in this [stereotyping]. For the attempt to see things
> freshly and in detail, rather than as types and generalities, is exhaust-
> ing, and among busy affairs this is practically out of the question....
> modern life is hurried and multifarious, and above all physical dis-
> tance separates men who are often in vital contact with each other,
> such as employer and employee, official and voter. There is neither
> time nor opportunity for intimate acquaintance. Instead we notice a
> trait which marks a well-known type, and fill in the rest of the pic-
> ture by means of the stereotypes we carry about in our heads. (71)

In this commentary on human nature and the impersonality of modern
political affairs, Lippmann notes that the nature of governance changes profoundly in reaction to the size of the community governed. The bigger we are, the
less we know of each other, and the more we depend on image and surface
impression to make up the difference. This, in turn, gives the mass media, which
either create or transmit most of our "stereotypes" about ourselves and each
other, a huge amount of control over the formation of public opinion and the construction of our social environment.

This notion of modern politics as a largely symbolic activity is explored by
Kurt and Gladys Lang (1966) in their important article, "The Mass Media and Voting." Extending ideas expressed by Lasswell and Cooley, the Langs observed that:

> It is the national news sources that largely serve to channel to the
> electorate the party image with the persistent symbols and cliches....
> We are also aware that most of what people know about political life

comes to them secondhand—or even third hand—through the mass media. The media do structure a very real political environment but one which, even in these days of television, we can only know "at a distance." (460–69)

Clearly, great political utility lies in using the mass media to stereotype political opponents and to mold public opinion regarding social events. Lippmann's idea of the "stereotype" as a coping mechanism by which busy voters organize unmanageable lives explains why the technique seems to work with people who ought to be impervious to such blatant manipulation. During the 1988 presidential election, for example, George Bush succeeded in tagging his opponent, Michael Dukakis, as a "liberal," and, by extension, as a "dove." Despite the fact that Dukakis's political record did not justify either of these two culturally ambivalent appellations, Bush's persistent and public reference to him as such lodged the image in the public mind. It also forced Dukakis to waste valuable time and money refuting Bush's description of him, lending even further credence to the theory that candidates who set the symbolic agenda also define the political playing grounds.

In terms of using the media to create public issues as well as to define political images, Lang and Lang (1966) point out that the media can be "part of the problem" instead of part of the solution, in that they play a perhaps unjustifiably predominant role in:

> ... filtering, structuring, and spotlighting certain [pre-election] public activities.... [the media] provide perspectives, shape images of candidates and parties, help highlight issues around which a campaign will develop, and define the unique atmosphere and areas of sensitivity which will mark any particular campaign. (462)

And, in taking their cue from the mass media, the public may find itself focusing on issues that are of secondary, tertiary, or even peripheral importance merely because the media have decided to focus on them first ... or, in a more sinister interpretation, because those ambitious figures who use the media as a tool for molding public thought have decided that a particular issue or set of issues would best suit their own political purposes. Such may be the power of the media, suggest the Langs (1966), that they can create:

> ... such definitions of overwhelming public sentiment—"landslide perceptions"—[that] tend to be cumulative. They influence political strategy; they inject a tone into news reporting; they seem to produce a certain reserve in personal discussion, since much conversation revolves around what is assumed to be held in common. (468)

A relevant case-in-point can be found in the highly profiled "war on drugs," an intensely publicized and enormously political social issue which was tossed about as a "hot potato" during the 1988 election. As Harold Lasswell (1966) puts it:

> The insecurities arising from the changes in the material environ-
> ment have been augmented by the stresses arising from the decline
> in potency of the older religious symbols and practices. Nationalism
> and [related cultural phenomena] are secularized alternatives to the
> surviving religious patterns, answering to the need of personalities
> to restabilize themselves in a mobile world. (39–40)

The operative phrase in this last quotation is "changes in the material envi-ronment." As Lasswell has pointed out previously, the political arena cannot be divorced from the social context in which it is properly located, and in great part that social environment depends for its tone and its texture on the economic infra-structure on which it rests. Marvin Harris (1987), I. M. Lewis (1976), and others have suggested that what lies below the surface of contemporary American soci-ety may be very different from what we see on top, while sociologists and politi-cal philosophers such as Karl Marx (1976), Fritz Pappenheim (1959), and Ferdinand Tonnies (Pappenheim 1959) have implied that this apparent crisis in our national intellectual health, this epidemic of political and social alienation, is the inevitable outcome when laissez-faire economic policies are coupled with unchecked technological expansion and deregulated private enterprise.

Alienation and political apathy

The question which follows logically from this is whether or not people living in late-20th century American society are experiencing more alienation than did their forerunners, and, if so, what implications that may have for political affairs. In addressing this issue, we must begin by understanding what is meant by the term "alienation."

Philosophical use of the word "alienation" must be credited to Ficte (1868, 1889) and Hegel (1974), who introduced the concept in the early 19th century. In the 1840s, Karl Marx (1976) appropriated it for use as a centerpiece concept in his work on the capitalist state, shifting the focus from a spiritual to an economic plane with his interpretation of the division between "natural" and "social" selves. Contemporary theologians, philosophers, and political theorists, such as Fritz Pappenheim (1959), have enlarged the traditional Marxian definition of "self-alienation" to accommodate all manner of personal estrangement and social confusion. And, with the advent of the "Information Age" in the 1980s, public awareness of the phenomenon itself seems to have reached a new level of concern, as American culture undergoes the most rapid and drastic change in its economic base since the time of the Industrial Revolution.

People have been talking about alienation—and about the cataclysmic world changes which it is perceived to accompany—since the invention of a language in which to voice their fears. To some degree, of course, societies are always "disintegrating," in the sense that they are mutating in response to the challenges, problems, and potential of their times. In some respects, they are not falling apart as much as they are metamorphosizing. In light of this pattern of growth and decline, is the claim that the twentieth century crisis differs from all the rest intellectually supportable? Anthropologist Marvin Harris (1987)—and despite his optimistic overview, philosopher Fritz Pappenheim (1959)—both say "yes."

Pappenheim traces alienation as a social phenomenon through 150 years of western history, using as his point of departure George Simmel's vision of the fundamental antagonism between "life" and "form." Put briefly, Simmel (1950, 1971) maintains that "pure" creative impulses, issuing from naive humanity, calcify into social conventions and cultural forms which then, ironically, inhibit the spontaneous expression of subsequent creative efforts.

This confrontational attitude toward social structures, in particular, achieves its most extreme expression in the existentialist schools of art, literature, and drama, in the work of "alienation ethics" writers such as Nietzsche (1924–74) and Kafka (1973), with their aggressive, exhausted despair. On a similarly cynical, but more hopeful note, are writers like Knut Hamsun (1920), who is sufficiently robust in his fractured way to condemn the purportedly "humanizing" elements of social organization without rejecting the possibility of eventual comfort. But throughout the work of all the writers and thinkers who fall somewhere along the existentialist continuum, there runs the common theme of human alienation, of estrangement, or inevitable and irreparable isolation. In their influence on humanity's dismal picture of the psychic world, these writers also impact the perceived viability of the democratic approach to self-government. And, as Lasswell (1966), Cooley (1966), and Harris (1987) might suggest, the existentialist message carries grave implications for the well-being of the democratic state.

For the social arena inevitably gives way onto political ground, and creating artificial distinctions among organically interconnected spheres of human experience is the first step toward creating a situation in which image wields more symbolic clout than does reality. Two World Wars, one Great Depression, one Great Inflation, a spate of assassinations, and a technological revolution have occurred since Simmel first wrote on the dangers of political alienation as a function of accelerated social change. And still the pace keeps picking up. With each new "breakthrough" in communications technology, with each new "revision" of the bureaucratic entities that govern our daily lives, with each new "refinement" of the various industrial techniques through which we pursue greater and greater "efficiency," we up the ante, we increase the demands made on the frail and tremulous psychic connections that make us feel, in some way, attached to each other and in control of ourselves. Marvin Harris (1987) describes the vociferous demands made on the modern "self" in economic terms.

> For the first time in history a whole generation of Americans despair of doing better than their parents. Not only are there relatively fewer middle-income families ($15,000 to $35,000 in constant 1982 dollars), but the income of those families in the age group 25–35 has dropped since 1965 from being equal to 96% of average family income to only 86%. And this has happened despite the fact that there are two wage earners in all these families where previously there was just one. (xviii)

George J. Church (1988), echoing this idea in the popular press, found that in 1988, the percentage of young people who could afford to buy their own homes dropped from 61 percent in 1978 to 53 percent in 1988—the lowest ebb yet since 1940. Since most down payments have come to require 50 percent of a full year's income, compared to the 33 percent needed in 1978, it isn't uprising that the young middle class is finding itself economically disenfranchised. For example, wages rose less than prices, during the 1980s, but not by much, and the average earning rate rose by just enough money to push the wage earner into a higher tax bracket—without the benefit of tax shelters that real estate offers to those in peak earning brackets. The result, as Church reports, is debt. During the year surrounding the 1988 election, fifty-five percent of all U.S. households owed more than what everything they owned was worth. And that's without considering the serious burden of the national debt, which if called to term in 1990 would have imposed a loss of at least $10,000 on each man, woman, and child counted in the most recent U.S. census—including infants and the homeless.

Compare this scenario with a U.S. Bureau of Statistics report broadcast by National Public Radio in October of 1988. The average Japanese citizen, so the federal report claimed, had, at that time, a savings account of $38,000, compared to the $15,000 that the average American had been able to sock away. In contrast, two Americans working in 1988 achieved about half of the buying power that one person working in 1982 had expected to enjoy—and that's assuming that both people in 1988 were earning 100 cents on the dollar, which they were not if one of them happened to be female. In that case, statistically, the female half of that economic unit pulled in between 50 percent and 70 percent of what the male half earned, despite the fact that her presence in the work force may have required them, as a couple, to hire alternative caretakers for themselves and for other members of their family unit. This, combined with the already depleted strength of the 1988 dollar, dragged their joint earning power down to somewhere between 25–35 percent of that enjoyed by a single white male, six years earlier.

Nor did the bad news about the American economy distribute evenly among income brackets or across racial lines. In a poll conducted by Gary Shilly, of the Yankelovich/*Time* research group (Church 1988, 28–30), fully 75 percent of America's rich (based on those who were polled) said that they'd gotten richer as a result of "Reaganomics," while 60 percent of the low-income Americans polled said that things had gotten worse. Blacks and the elderly reported the most severe deterioration of their economic health, at rates of 43 percent and 50 percent, respectively. And, according to the U.S. Congressional Budget Office (U.S. Congress 1987), the poorest 10 percent of America's population actually lost ground in terms of real dollars and cents; in 1977 they pulled in an average of $3,673.00 each, but in 1988, they only managed to clear $3,286.00. The wealthiest five percent of our population, on the other hand, went from an average earning of $94,476.00 to $129,762 in that same eleven-year time span.

Given this dismal economic landscape, it's not unexpected that America's consumers, who are also America's voters, should fall prey to the first ravages of social despair. Compounding their economic burdens were—are—the psychic drains inflicted by living in an essentially hostile urban world, defined most conspicuously by the bureaucratic model of public management. Buried under mountains of paperwork, Harris (1987) implies, the human spirit cannot long endure without resorting to anger, and when anger becomes too much of an effort, the psychological fibers and sociological bonds that hold us together, separately and in our primary groups, begin to fray, start to unravel. And social despair, combined with moral fatigue and the erosion of cultural will, dissolves into political alienation.

Political alienation is not a new thing. But as Harris (1987) and Pappenheim (1959) suggest, the quality and the quantity of the phenomenon in contemporary American politics may very well be unprecedented.

This thought evokes Ferdinand Tonnies' (1940, 1957) classic works on the different types of human community, which Tonnies divides into two main groupings. A "Gesellschaft" society, claims Tonnies, is essentially contractual in nature. People relate to each other according to function; they enjoy only limited personal contacts, defined by shared social boundaries or common operational needs. In contrast, people living in a "Gemeinschaft" society relate to each other as whole individuals, rather than as fragments of such; the community is held together by emotional bonds exceeding contractual arrangement. Gemeinschaft societies are truly cohesive; Gesellschaft communities, on the surface at least, are modelled sheerly along lines of functional convenience. As a large, highly industrialized, intensely bureaucratic state, the United States falls into the category of a Gesellschaft society, although smaller, Gemeinschaft communities may continue to exist within the broader national description.

Tonnies seems to feel that Gemeinschaft communities are by far the more pleasant place in which to live, since they nurture human existence on the emotional as well as on the substantive level. Certainly Marvin Harris (1987) would agree with this assumption, since he places much of the blame for what he perceives as a dangerously high degree of cultural frustration on the 20th century burgeoning of state and corporate bureaucracy. The impersonality of these bureaucratized relationships may become internalized within the individual, one may infer, much like victims of child abuse internalize the damaged self-image which is foisted upon them by those who should be looking after their welfare. The subsequent loss of self-esteem, in both situations, is reflected in the individual's attitude toward himself or herself, as well as in the development of strained relations between the individual and the social group.

The routinization of human relationships creates a situation in which human beings relate in terms of images rather than realities. If the Langs' work is placed within the social context described by Marx and Tonnies, it becomes quickly apparent that an inordinate amount of power—both hidden and overt—is wielded by the mass media in an alienated, industrialized, Geselleschaft society like the contemporary United States, as Marvin Harris (1987) characterizes that nation. This realization goes a long way toward clarifying the reasons why people might choose to elect a leader who, economically, at least, does not seem to be performing in their own best interests.

"Tonnies' fears," notes Pappenheim (1959):

> ... were borne out in a tragic way in the 1930's, when Hitler and his followers, imbued with their idea of national Gemeinschaft, attempted to reverse the direction in which German life was moving.... these efforts, [feared Tonnies], could produce only artificial facades, empty forms, which instead of serving the forces of life and furthering their growth would stifle and destroy them. (69)

Once the shift toward Gesellschaft is launched, it must then be acknowledged institutionally. Only then can the social changes which it ushers in be dealt with in a realistic and constructive fashion. Ignoring these changes opens the door to dangerous manipulation of the masses by political forces, since the emotion which was grounded previously in real community roots is separated from its organic base and made available for application wherever it may be most useful. The presence of mass media as a defining influence in the development of cultural perceptions contributing to either type of state—Gemeinschaft or Geselleschaft—can be, unfortunately, misleading. As Gunther Andres (Pappenheim 1959) writes:

> [As a result of television and radio] ... events come to us, not we to them. We no longer feel the immediate and physical results of our

actions. And this makes us sloppy. When both action and individual
are obscured in a general mire of moral unaccountability, the rules
of the social game alter drastically. (106)

To review, then, we have explored the relationship between political symbols and the social environment in which they occur, focusing on probable causes
of increasing alienation among voters and the role which that may subsequently
play in their perception of changing community structures and related social realities. Two broad historical trends—the shift from a Gemeinschaft to a
Gesellschaft society and the ascension of the mass media as a force for creating
social imagery and shaping political thought—have been identified as important
features of these two trends. But the question still remains as to what type of cat-
alyst may be required to bring all this together in a way which yields the kind of
profound political upheaval seen in the 1980 presidential election and maintained
throughout the 1984 and 1988 contests. In their work on the role and nature of
symbolic leadership in the post-industrialized state, Max Weber (1968) and Orrin
Klapp (1964) have some light to shed on this issue.

Symbolic leaders in the Geselleschaft state

The American voting public, in 1988, was perhaps more alienated than at any
other time in its social history, a condition which, in turn, invited manipulation of
political thought through the creation and transmission of political imagery via
the mass media. Foremost among the "images" involved in any political campaign, of course, are the images of the candidates themselves.

Orrin Klapp (1964) has done some interesting work on types of symbolic
leaders, in which he concludes that an alienated population is more prone to seiz-
ing upon symbolic, as opposed to "real" or functionally operative, leaders than
are people living in a society in which citizens feel that they have a direct and
vital role in governing the community. He goes on to point out that communities
in crisis, or societies in which profound cultural changes are occurring, often
don't know what they want in terms of political leadership until well-defined
options are set before them. It is much easier to choose than to create.

In their 1988 choice of a president, the American people selected a leader
who symbolized the political denial of any social more complex or deep-rooted
than drug addiction. George Bush's 1988 campaign rhetoric denied, flat out, that
America was in trouble. Perhaps he inherited this convenient myopia from
Ronald Reagan, for whom it worked like a charm for years. What is important is
the realization that, by their repeated endorsement of the Republican leaders, the
American people seemed to prefer this dangerous type of tunnel vision to a clear
look at the hard facts.

Klapp (1964), Pappenheim (1959), and Tonnies (1957) might reply that
voters dodge the difficult truths of their time because they simply can't handle

them, because they are too alienated, too exhausted, because they don't know what they want and they're too frightened to admit that what they used to want isn't possible to have anymore. So they deny the evidence of their own eyes, and follow the leader who promises to bring back the "good life," whose vision of the future most closely resembles the idealized memory of the past, in which the United States was a clean, honorable, *solvent*, Gemeinschaft place to live. Indeed, at the heart of the Bush attack on Dukakis was the accusation that the Governor was a "cold," "rational," "intellectual" man, who made decisions based on fact rather than on feeling.

Klapp (1964) raises the point that, over time, symbolic leaders can become "institutionalized," cementing themselves into place as a kind of billboard for perceived cultural values. This permits their originally ephemeral influence to concretize, resulting in a type of symbolic commodity which can be transferred from one symbolic leader to another, as long as that which they symbolize remains consistent in the public eye. One type of leader who straddles both the symbolic and functional dimensions of public governance is the "charismatic leader" described by sociologist Max Weber.

Charisma and symbolic leadership

Weber (1968) describes "charisma" as a temporary authority which has at its root a spontaneous, personal, almost mystic connection between charismatic leaders and the people whom they lead. He describes the link between charismatic leaders and their followers as direct, dynamic, and unmediated by institutional forces. Connections between the charismatic leader and the source of his or her authority are similarly immediate and unimpeded—power is attributed to visions, to magic, to the "gift of grace," as exemplified by the leader's achievement of extraordinary feats. According to Weber, charismatic leaders demonstrate their fitness for office through their own "strength in life," and the people whom they lead monitor their continued qualifications for the job because they enjoyed sustained and continued access to them. Glassman and Swatos (1986) note the emotionally charged nature of charismatic leadership:

> ... the charismatic leader may emerge as a religious prophet, a war leader, or a great orator. In each of these spheres, human anxiety can run high, while signs from "The Beyond" attain increasing significance. We can, in a broad sense, then, agree with Karl Lowenstein when he observes that (fundamentally) ... the locus of charisma is in the world of religion. (3)

Glassman and Swatos go on to note that "Although Weber recognized significant differences between the institutional spheres of the military, politics, and religion, he was also careful not to divorce them" (4). This remark has great significance relative to a discussion of the Reagan Administration's "war on drugs," without which the Bush election strategy would not have seized upon the issue with quite the same ferocity as it did.

Edward Shils (Glassman and Swatos 1986) comments that the term "charisma" may have been devalued by its frequent and imprecise use. He cautions against labelling leaders as "charismatic" merely because they are popular. Shils' point is well taken, but enough evidence has accrued to suggest that the Reagan Administration did operate along lines which could be called "charismatic" in the Weberian sense of the word. Perhaps the strongest case-in-point along these lines is the so-called "Teflon Man" metaphor of the first Reagan term, in which a President seemed to enjoy spectacular degree of *un*accountability for one political disaster after another.

Perhaps this political sorcery can be attributed, at least in part, to the fact that in the late twentieth century charismatic leaders can still claim authority based on past heroic deeds, without having to be factually accountable, since the public can no longer monitor the verity of their claims. The direct pipeline between those who lead and those who are led has become clogged with mediated imagery, choked with manipulated symbols. To some degree, Weber's own work (1968) on the concept of "depersonalized charisma" foreshadowed this situation.

The phenomenon of depersonalized charisma, as Weber explains it, is a kind of spiritual commodity, the assignment of property rights, as were, to the earned and spontaneous charisma described in his earlier work. The most important thing about "depersonalized charisma" is that it can be transferred from one leader to another, much as Orrin Klapp (1964) describes "cultural resonance" as something which can be passed from one symbolic leader to another. George Bush's early and public status as heir apparent to the Republican White House would be an example of this principle in action. But depersonalized charisma is difficult to maintain, propped up as it is on bits and pieces of borrowed glamour. The most frequent support system through which modern depersonalized charisma is sustained are the mass media. As Glassman and Swatos (1966) note:

> The manufacture of charisma through the mass media creates a whole new category of leadership, carrying a pseudocharismatic aura. In modern social-technical settings, even a genuine charismatic leader would have to seek the enhancing devices of the mass media to broaden the charismatic effect into a mass phenomenon of an all-encompassing kind. Hitler, ironically, was the first modern charismatic leader to utilize the mass media in this way. However, leaders lacking genuine charisma will turn to the mass media in order to attempt to manufacture pseudocharisma in its place. Though this manufactured charisma does not create the same cathetic bond that

genuine charisma generates in the charismaterized followers, it does
create an aura of ever-present recognition and "star" status. (6)

The most chilling modern example of mass seduction by a charismatic
leader is provided by the case of Adolf Hitler and the rise of the Nazi Party in pre-
World War Two Germany. Weber died before Hitler's rise to power was complete,
but Glassman and Swatos (1966), Edward Shils (Glassman and Swatos 1966),
and Orrin Klapp (1964) have all noted many similarities between Joseph Goebbels' skillful rendering of Hitler as a national savior of 1930s Germany and the
techniques by which present-day media images are made. This exceptional inci-
dent in world affairs contains some important clues about the successful manu-
facture of what Weber calls "depersonalized charisma" and its potential effect on
national politics.

Ernest K. Bramsted's study (1965) of Nazi propaganda draws on the diaries and correspondence of Goebbels, Hitler, Himmler, Goring, and other Party
luminaries to depict German domestic strategy in promoting Hitler as a world-
class charismatic leader. The first factor, claims Bramsted (1965), was the
"...total scope (of the propaganda effort), the fact that it was not confined to the
political sphere, but that it extended to the whole range of cultural activities of the
nation" (53). The second step was to keep tabs on the national mood, or as Goebbels himself put it, to "be close to the people, to know where their shoe pinches."
This assured that the information churned out by the propaganda machine had
cultural or economic relevance for the population at any given time, an early
example of marketing strategy, one, might say, carried out on a national scale.

Once the marketing research was done, operationalization could occur.
Again, Goebbels' diaries (Bramsted 1965) provide a concise account of his rules
for performing public relations wizardry on behalf of his "Fuhrer."

The first rule was to never tell a complete lie. Instead, Goebbels advised
his staff to devise new ways of "interpreting" facts and events to make them more
advantageous to the Party image. Second, he insisted, keep things simple. The
more naturally complex a social problem, the more simple a solution for solving
it should be suggested; hence, in part, the alacrity with which scapegoating the
Jews was seized upon as a cure-all for Germany's many economic woes. Third,
Goebbels counseled his staff and underlings to remember that the public, in his
view, had an amazingly short and selective memory, and that anything said often
enough and loudly enough would eventually come to be believed. But perhaps
the most striking "accomplishment" of Goebbels' regime was his success in por-
traying Adolf Hitler as a demigod who also shared human traits with his fellow—
albeit lesser—Germans.

In this regard, Goebbels' strategy could be straight out of Weber's description (1968) of the truly charismatic leader. In his ability to position Hitler as the
"fulfillment of a mysterious national longing" (Bramsted 1965, 199), the

Propaganda Minister fanned economic fear into nationalistic fervor, invoking a quasi-religious loyalty to the man whom Germans came to perceive as their ethnic "Everyman" as much as their military messiah. He did this by beginning with the fringe elements of German society, gradually moving them into the mainstream of national politics as their economic base became increasingly secure.

"In his pseudo-missionary jargon," Goebbels mobilized "small but determined minorities," who pounded the German countryside extolling Hitler's virtues as the embodiment of essential German values (Bramsted 1965). These political zealots were by and large of two types—older, traditional folk, who longed for the simple answers of an earlier age, and young firebrands, seeking to resurrect the militant, unified Germany about which they heard so much and experienced so little. In the middle ground stood the confused bulk of the German people, still bruised from relatively recent military defeat in the First World War and battered by the severe economic deprivations which accompanied it. The time was ripe for demagoguery, and the Nazi Party had a perfect candidate in the awful, eloquent Adolf Hitler.

Perhaps one of Goebbels' cleverest ploys was depicting Hitler as a warm, caring human being who just happened to have been touched by the divine hand of destiny. In a pre-election flurry of newspaper articles singing Hitler's human praises, Goebbels' helped to fuel the Nazi drive to Party leadership in 1933. He described Hitler as an artist, as a humble man, whom "only the misery of the German people had called into politics" (Bramsted 1965, 203). This sugar-coated journalistic treatment distinguished Hitler from his many rivals for control of the Reich Stag, cloaking his personal thirst for power behind an unselfish "call" from a higher source. Again, shades of Weber's divinely propelled charismatic leader come to mind.

No one is suggesting here that George Bush was in any substantive way an evil man reminiscent of Adolf Hitler. But the parallels between Nazi Party propaganda strategy in 1933 and the Republican Party media campaign in the 1980s are striking, beginning with the 1980 claim that the newly elected team of Ronald Reagan and George Bush had been given a "mandate" by the American people, continuing through to George Bush's 1988 image as just a "regular, friendly guy," and extending all the way into the 1992 campaign being positioned as a "cultural war" against Bill Clinton. And, as Walter Shapiro (1988c) and other political journalists have commented, Bush's "media handlers" took great care to bill him as a normal, all-American "family man."

Max Weber's work (1968) on the phenomenon of charisma and its impact on emerging political movements suggests that contemporary world leaders must somehow achieve the "larger-than-life," super-enhanced stature of which Adolf Hitler was such a chilling example. Whether such stature can still develop naturally, or whether we have reached such an advanced state of Gesellschaft that it must needs be pursued primarily through manipulation of the mass media, is an

interesting question which is still very much open to debate. But Weber's observation that, in either instance, the charismatic leader must cite some higher
authority as the source of his right to govern, is a critical one, since it ties in
directly with the Reagan-Bush "mandate" of 1980, the 1992 "cultural war" trum-
peted by Dan Quayle, Pat Buchanan, and their supporters, and what anthropologist Marvin Harris (1987) calls the "Third Great Awakening" of American
spiritualism—and the intrusion of that religious sensibility into the realm of
American national politics.

Weber originally framed charisma as a transitional type of authority. But
the ability of the mass media to preserve political symbolism, coupled with long-
term propaganda strategizing on the part of political special-interest groups, has
introduced a state of affairs in which Weber's old, almost anti-authoritarian brand
of "pure charisma" may take a permanent back seat to the "depersonalized"
model. Neatly packaged and labelled for network distribution, depersonalized
charisma has a shelf life that lasts for as long as its sponsors can afford to fund it.
This loosens up the time frame of political strategies, allowing for a game plan
based on a longer lead time than the actual lifespan of any single political leader.
Most importantly, perhaps, media-produced and transmitted symbols can be used
to keep political campaigning in motion between as well as within election years,
since public support is no longer linked to a single individual and partisan loyal-
ties are no longer limited to expressly political concerns. Support can be
"whipped up" and maintained for a whole range of related issues, as long as they
harken back, eventually, to the fundamental symbolism vested in the character of
the original depersonalized charismatic leader.

One of the more useful strategies for eliciting long-term support for a depersonalized or media-manufactured charismatic leader, as Goebbels fully realized, is through the timely creation of a "holy war" or a similarly attractive moral
crusade. "Jihads," as such efforts are sometimes termed, provide a convenient
means by which public attention can be diverted from internal problems and public hostility can be levied against a socially exogenous scapegoat. Goebbels, of
course, had the Jews—and every one else who didn't fit the Nazi vision of a puri-
fied Aryan race. In writing about America's return to religion as a way of
addressing both secular and spiritual problems, a look at the political utility of
holy wars supplies an interesting framework for the understanding the intense
dynamics of the 1988 presidential race.

Holy wars have long provided human beings with a way to organize patterns of relative morality within and between different groups in society. For
western thinkers, perhaps, the term itself invokes images of Islamic religious
ferocity, typified by the phenomenon of the "Jihad." But we can conjure up near
relatives of the Jihad fairly close to home, discerning within the social evolution of
recent Western history "holy wars" of varying intensity, duration, and social target,
ranging from medieval crusades, to New England witch hunts, to Prohibition, to

the terrible reign of the Third Reich, to the McCarthyism of the 1950s. Granted, these events cover a wide range of moral territory, and are far more complex in social and economic terms than simple functional comparisons can convey. But they, too, contributed to the maintenance of social control within their respective historical periods, in the same way that the jihad dominates its time and place.

One important trait common to all holy wars is that they shift public attention to a convenient out-group rather than allowing it rest on various short-comings of the political group in power at the time when the "war" takes place. Beginning with the notion of "possession" by evil spirits and progressing to modern-day attitudes concerning drug use and addiction, holy wars have proven to be the most effective when converts can unite against an entity perceived to be so alien, or against an intrusion so outrageously foreign, that moral indignation can be aroused and the concept of redemption for various types of "sinners" or "victims" can be invoked. In the 1980s, addiction *per se* was positioned as this kind of alien presence.

In a biting commentary on the social drift toward a "clean and sober" society, anthropologist Thomas Szasz (1974) hints at the emergence of a collective obsession with "cleansing" oneselfÆ—and one's entire society—from the malignant presence of all chemical substances. Linked to the biologically polluting nature of drugs and alcohol, suggests Szasz, is some important moral freight, including the implicit assumption that drug use and alcoholism, either one's own or another's, is in some way responsible for any and all childhood misfortune or adult-life character deficiency. One's actual degree of chemical dependency does not matter in this *ad hoc* moral assessment. In the cosmology of the chemically righteous, claims Szasz, there is no such thing as a "social drinker." There are only latent alcoholics who have not yet recognized their alcoholism; there are only sinners who remain yet to be saved. The religious connotations are intentional, for in the "Alcoholics Anonymous" mindframe, as in born-again Christianity, salvation is an all-or-nothing proposition. Either one is reformed, or one is not. And if one is not saved, then one is damned, lost, or diseased. It is this very sense of righteousness that makes the "clean and sober" movement, as well as the "war on drugs," such politically volatile phenomena, since it is the promise of redemption that adds zest to any crusade. And once a "holy war" is launched, it is frighteningly easy to maintain, and frighteningly easy to re-direct for blatantly political purposes. Intolerance is the keynote in campaigns of moral indignation, and intolerance and freedom of speech do not go hand in hand. There are no broad-minded zealots.

This is not to suggest that drug addiction, itself, is an American civil liberty, or that the abuse of drugs is something which ought to be defended. The concern, here, is with the political utility intrinsic in any sustained national crisis, as demonstrated by how the "war on drugs" has been politically positioned and waged. What is troubling about the "clean and sober" movement is its intolerance for the exercise of free choice among those who elect to use alcohol responsibly. Similar alarm about the "war on drugs" revolves not around the tolerance of drug use and drug-related crime, but rather around the governmental leeway which public fear about drugs has permitted to flourish, and about the ethical and legislative latitude which the supposed gravity and magnitude of the drug problem has purchased for government entities. In 1988, the "war on drugs," to some extent, provided a perfect politically expedient red herring for the Reagan-Bush brand of Republicanism; if getting fired up about drugs distracted even a small percentage of voters from thinking hard thoughts about the Administration's ineffectiveness in dealing with economic and diplomatic problems, then the "war" was a success, albeit in a covert arena.

What historical parallels might be able to shed some light on this contemporary phenomena? Three functionally similar constellations of historical event present themselves. In a broad sense, the scapegoating of supposed "witches" in early American and in other societies provides some insight into the mechanisms by which "holy war" distractions can operate. A brief look at the way in which the European Crusades managed to achieve political unity in pursuit of supposedly "moral" goals supplies a basis of comparison for the techniques by which disparate elements in American political parties can be brought to rally around a central symbolic issue. And, in a more specific sense, the American Prohibition movement of the early 20th century supplies concrete comparisons with contemporary attitudes toward intoxicating or "possessive" substances and their impact on American social life.

Sir James Frazer (1935) writes of the ubiquitous presence of evil "demons" in human societies ranging from the pre-tribal to the imperial. Like Marvin Harris (1987) and Thomas Szasz (1974), he cites the periodic expulsion of evil as a routine function in human social life, comparing Greek and Roman Saturnalia festivals with the surviving Christian custom of Lent. Particularly interesting is Frazer's assertion that scapegoating, in one form or another, is an enduring human instinct, fraught with potential for political application. He maintains that the scapegoating process is immensely useful to the dominant elite in any given society, both as a mechanism for maintaining a general level of social control and as a psychological device for transferring burdens of economic failure from the social to the theological realms.

In *Cows, Pigs, Wars, and Witches*, Marvin Harris (1978) supplies a succinct illustration of Frazer's point:

> The principal result of the [Inquisition] witch-hunt system (aside from charred bodies) was that the poor came to believe that they were being victimized by witches and devils instead of by princes and popes.... Against the people's phantom enemies, Church and state mounted a bold campaign. The authorities were unstinting in

their efforts to ward off this evil, and rich and poor alike could be thankful for the energy and bravery displayed in the battle. (205)

Harris notes that this gratitude on the part of the frightened public seemed to exist despite the fact that the religious and secular officials who were fighting the "battle" were also rewarded handsomely for their efforts by confiscating the property of the condemned. An added bonus, for both 16th century and 20th century guardians of public morality, is the suspension of normal civil liberties that an atmosphere of national crisis seems to justify. As LaPierre (1954) puts it in his work on the psychological foundations of social control:

> ... adversity breeds caution, a revival and revitalization of the tried and true. It therefore provides an opportunity for those in positions of authority—politicians, business leaders, etc.—to extend their powers.... Widespread social adversity gives rise to such "purification" measures as witch hunting, "red baiting," and drives against crime, vice, another deviant forms of social conduct. (533)

If witch hunting gives people under duress something to think about besides their own problems, a crusade supplies them with a common foe against whom they can close ranks. In a perverse kind of way, "holy wars" bring people together. They define the social group to itself and to those whom it marks as "outsiders." And crusades supply dissident or dissatisfied elements within a society with a "big idea," with a larger cause for which to fight. Additionally, crusades can camouflage private ambition in the cloak of patriotic duty or religious ardor.

In his study of 13th century public opinion and crusade propaganda, Palmer A. Throop (1940) concludes that the "real" Crusades served a number of inter-related social functions, several of which were economic in concern. For one thing, they redirected the public's attention, shifting the focus of concern away from less popular—and more morally complicated—domestic policies, like the continued and excessive tithing of dirt-poor peasants. They also reinforced the then-useful perception that papal authority was, in some deep moral sense, superior to that of the many kings and petty nobles who were fighting for control of Europe's fragmented political landscape. But the most important cultural use of the Crusades, claims Throop, was their temporarily unifying effect on their squabbling, brawling European nation-states—an artificial bonding which lasted, as he notes, only as long as the Church was able to sustain the illusion that the Crusades, despite the military and economic hardships which they imposed on the population, were a winning proposition embarked upon for the good of Europe's collective soul. Once it became apparent that the Holy Wars benefited the Church more than they did the church-goers, and once the aggregate

European congregation finally rebelled against the tremendous tax burdens required to fund an ongoing foreign war, popular support for the Holy Wars disintegrated. The Crusades, says Throop, then collapsed under their own weight, much as the American crusade against alcohol collapsed during the 1930s from the enormous expense involved in trying to administer unenforceable drinking laws.

Two things about the American Prohibition movement are particularly alarming in light of Bramsted's discoveries (1965) about frightened people in groups and their scapegoating tendencies. First, Prohibition was forced upon a culturally shell-shocked American public by a small relatively small group of morally zealous extremists. It did not come out of "mainstream" America, yet it influenced the public actions and the private habits of every American citizen for almost 14 years (Sinclair 1964). Second, it re-introduced into the 20th century the idea of "possession" by malignant internal forces over which the individual had no control. Prohibition substituted the idea of disease for the older concept of demon. It linked the achievement of moral well-being with factors residing outside of the particular human being whose health was at stake, re-assigning the responsibility for the maintenance of public morality to social institutions, rather than allowing it to remain a private duty. In terms of allocating responsibility for psychic well-being, Prohibition reversed Martin Luther's re-empowerment of the individual. In this way, Prohibition can be seen as a precursor to the current "war on drugs"—and the civil dangers inherent in the patronizing moral attitudes of the Prohibitionist movement presage the equally dangerous paternalistic attitudes of the Reagan Administration toward drug use in American society.

Let's look first at the idea that Prohibition played a role in the United States of the 1930s similar to the role played by witch hunting in 13th century Europe, and then go on to consider the implications of medicalizing what are, conceptually speaking, demonic forces.

In his social history of the Prohibition movement, Andrew Sinclair (1964) notes that the "dry crusade" emerged during a period of profound social upheaval. Americans living in the early part of the 20th century were confronted with the twin specters of escalating industrialization and mass immigration by hordes of unskilled workers from Eastern Europe. Added to this was the political ferment accompanying women's suffrage. Every aspect of "traditional" American life was under either real or perceived assault. As Sinclair points out, the political fallout from this unprecedented constellation of social circumstances tended to group along extreme lines. One option, which reinforces Marx's (1976), Tonnies' (Pappenheim 1959), and Pappenheim's (1959) theories regarding the political consequences of social alienation, was apathy. When women's vote groups linked up with rabid nationalists to proclaim the dangers posed by "demon rum" to a gentle, considerate, sexually equitable and racially pure America, most people didn't buy it, but they were too tired, and too bombarded by the psychological assaults of their time, to protest. Then, too, many people just didn't take the Prohibitionists seriously enough until it was too late (Sinclair 1964). As in the 1980s, the climate of repressed but profound social anxiety provided the perfect emotional setting in which to stage a moral coup. As Sinclair (1964) remarks:

> The 18th Amendment could not have passed without the support of the psychologically tolerant, made temporarily intolerant [by the stress of war and the threat of profound social change]. (23)

And, he goes on to note, once the "dry" crusade gained enough social momentum to influence political affairs, national leaders seized upon the phenomenon as a useful campaign tool, as a device for gaining or maintaining moral leverage on "the other guy." Here again, parallels can be drawn between Prohibition as a political opportunity and the "war on drugs" as a symbolic stump on which the 1988 presidential candidates stood, the better to hurl labels at one another.

Another shared feature of witch-hunting, Prohibition, and the "war on drugs" is extremism. Sinclair (1964) notes:

> The real tragedy of the prohibitionist ideology was that it left no room for temperance. The dry crusade slipped slowly from a moderate remedy for obvious evils into a total cure-all for society. The creed of the dedicated dry would not admit the existence of the moderate drinker. By definition, all drinkers were bound to become alcoholics.... The doctrine of prohibition appealed to the psychology of excess, both in its friends and its foes.... The fight against the devil carries another devil in its exaggerations. With a consecrated prejudice on the part of the drays and an unenlightened self-interest on the part of the wets, there was little room left for compromise. (28–29)

In describing this early version of "Zero Tolerance," Sinclair leads naturally into the work of Thomas Szasz (1974), who traces the development of the contemporary idea of drug use as an "addiction" rather than as a "vice." As Szasz (1974) notes, the Prohibitionist vision of alcohol as something which seizes control of its "victims'" entire moral being has been imported wholesale by the righteous attitudes of contemporary crusaders. This can lead to extreme moves on the part of government that would not otherwise be tolerated.

The gist of Szasz's argument (1974) is that drugs provide the political elite with a "safe" social ill over which to wax both eloquent and righteous. No politician in his or her right mind would seriously argue that drug abuse is a good thing. But it is the illegality of drugs, not their use, which is of greatest use in the political arena, argues Szasz, and his point is backed up by his colleague James W. Brown (1974), who cites the sordid story of the 1965 New York city mayoral election as a case in point.

It began, claim Brown *et al.*, when the then mayor of New York, John Lindsay, realized that he might be able to squeeze some much-needed political leverage from spreading public money throughout various social agencies dealing with narcotics use and abuse in the "Big Apple." Lindsay "proved" his concern about the city's drug problem by spending the city's money on fruitless research and expensive limited-population clinics. The 1965 mayoral election saw both Republicans and Democrats batting responsibility for the drug problem all over the municipal arena, since Lindsay had set the political agenda for the race by isolating drug abuse as a symbol of the city's moral decay. Outrageous campaign rhetoric was delivered by both sides in thundering tones—such as the statement that more than half of violent crimes committed in New York were related to drug abuse, a claim contradicted by the official police statistics for that year, which set the figure at about five percent.

Eventually, Lindsay won the election, largely on the grounds that both liberals and moderates supported his anti-drug policies. Consequently, one of his first mayoral acts was to establish the Addiction Services Agency (ASA), an umbrella organization for the many smaller groups battling drug abuse on the "front lines." In the way of big city agencies, the ASA quickly became bogged down in paperwork and bureaucracy, and—after sinking more than half a billion dollars into it—even Lindsay was forced to concede that his brainchild was ill-conceived and even more ill-administered. He lost the next election for governor to Rockefeller, in great part because of the political credibility—and the city revenues—he had squandered in his own "war on drugs." Lots of money was spent, writes Brown (1974), making a lot of drug therapists, counselors, law enforcement officials, medical doctors, social scientists, and de-toxification bureaucrats very happy. But little was accomplished that really helped the truly addicted. And just about nothing was done to help the rest of the people of New York, who thought that they were voting to spend money in the right place when they voted for John Lindsay. New Yorkers still had the same high crime rate, the same creeping cultural erosion, the same soaring cost of living, the same disintegrating quality of life, as they had before they threw away half a billion dollars on their new drug "rehab" program. And that would have happened even if the ill-fated ASA had been an efficient, dynamic organization, maintains Brown (1974), because drug abuse was not the real cause of the city's entire litany of social problems in the first place.

America's drug problem, as Brown (1974), Szasz (1974), and Marvin Harris (1987) suggest, is really symptomatic of a larger complex of social ills, both cultural and economic at root, which cannot be collapsed into a single diagnosis or cured with a single prescription. But it is not presented that way, because it is far more politically expedient for the powers that be to present drugs as the cause, rather than as the result, of an ailing economic system and the deteriorating cultural fabric in which it is wrapped. As long as drugs can be held up as the national villain, the solution to American problems can be made to seem simple, unattainable, and relatively swift. It is far easier to jail, fine, electrocute, and deport drug traffickers than it is to undertake the massive social reforms and economic adjustments that Harris (1987) and others suggest are necessary if the current quality of American life can be maintained, let alone improved.

The point is an important one, since it suggests that fear about specific social concerns can prompt American voters into throwing away their moral autonomy in exchange for social reassurance. What cannot be controlled through legislation can, perhaps, be "conquered" by re-definition. As Szasz (1974) somewhat cynically implies, as a culture the United States has become addicted to the idea of addiction, thus absolving itself of the responsibility to exercise rational control over behavior. Compulsion is excusable where failures of moral character are not. Addicts, by definition, cannot "help" what they do, any more than witches, according to 13th century doctrine, could be "saved" from eternal damnation an appeal to their power of reason. No one wants to be an addict, presumably, any more than some one would want to be a damned soul, so the burden falls upon society to save those poor wretches who cannot save themselves. And so potent is the threat of forces which cause individuals to act against their own best interests that any measure required to combat these enemies is seen as justifiable, no matter how harsh, no matter how presumptive, no matter how irreconcilable that measure may be with the essential spirit of enlightened self-government.

This move to create a sense of national emergency, and to coax away from the American electorate the power to make moral decisions, is clearly evident in the Republican campaign rhetoric of the 1988 presidential election. A comparison of the political philosophies of the two candidates, as revealed by analysis of their pre-election propaganda, indicates that the forces of social history discussed throughout this chapter have come together in the contemporary political arena, converging in a particularly virulent fashion as the intrusion of moral righteousness in more properly secular spheres.

Leadership style and political philosophy

Set against the technologized Gesellshaft society of the late 20th century, political leaders who appeal to the public's need for emotional comfort and spiritual solace can use the mass media to polish their "depersonalized" charisma to an even glossier shine. As noted by Orrin Klapp (1964), and as exploited by Joseph Goebbels (Bramsted 1965), the image of a sort of "national family" is extremely useful in this regard. Symbolic fatherhood is an immensely marketable commodity in the type of confused, anxious political landscape described by Harris

(1987) and Tonnies (Pappenheim 1959). Republican campaign rhetoric during the 1988 elections exploited this fact.

What distinguished the 1988 election from its recent peers was the presence of two candidates with well-defined and diametrically opposing positions on a range of important social issues. Despite press accusations that 1988 was an "issueless" campaign, the two presidential hopefuls stated their views on real social concerns, clearly, succinctly, and often. And their views were very different, presenting the American public with some real choices to make on their November ballots.

George Bush swept into office with the first Reagan victory in 1980, one of the notably few survivors of that early entourage. Bush was above all else a team player, a company man. Intimates called him "nice," "overwhelmingly nice," a "nice, loyal kind of guy," a cog to be counted on in the Republican Party machinery (Shapiro 1988c, 18–20). Critics implied that Bush's "niceness" crossed the line between amiability and amorality, that he was more concerned with propping up the conservative platform as a means of advancing his own career than he was with facing tough issues and making decisions about those issues based on his own real convictions. During the 1988 election, both Bush and the Grand Old Party (GOP) lined up behind traditional, well-entrenched conservative values, such as God, family, law and order, economic expansion, and military strength. The Democratic forces met Bush on common symbolic ground, building their own campaign strategy around the same set of iconic elements. Differences lay in the philosophical perspectives with which the two parties approached the same political turf, but the ground covered was essentially the same. The cognitive approaches used to address these issues, however, differed radically between candidates.

Both parties claimed to pursue the same objectives—cleaning up the national debt, strengthening America's military capability, getting the U.S. economy back on track, wiping out drug abuse as a national problem, preserving Social Security, and addressing the homeless issue. Yet each party maintained, assiduously, that the other was completely out of touch with the desires and concerns of "mainstream America." Strategically, these reciprocal accusations of distortion were necessary in order to create a marketable distinction between the two sets of similar political goals, since party public relations experts on both sides realized that objectives are easier to market than are ideologies. And the contrasting sales rhetoric used to sell these objectives to the voting public betrayed a marked difference in philosophical attitudes between the two candidates.

For example, both candidates, to return to an earlier theme, cited the need to clamp down on criminal drug use as an urgent social concern. George Bush's prescription for dealing with the problem revolved around the implementation of emergency enforcement measures, and included executing drug dealers, among other punitive methods. Dukakis also advocated getting "tough on drugs," but stressed the need for education and similar preventive strategies in lieu of expanding police powers and invoking the death penalty. Bush's approach was expressly paternalistic; the hidden message was: "Let government make these hard choices and carry out these difficult tasks for you." Dukakis's meta-message implied a greater faith in the power of the educated individual to do what is "right;" buried within his rhetoric on this issue was the idea that the appropriate role of the government is to give to the governed the tools they need to make their own decisions. Dukakis's political philosophy was classically post-Enlightenment; Bush's, in the Weberian (1968) sense, was more aligned with the post-industrial charismatic model of leadership.

Similarly, the candidates' diametrically opposing stands on the abortion issue revealed their contrasting attitudes about people's ability to make their own moral choices. Dukakis was not pro-abortion. His opponents claimed that he was, but in doing so they deliberately smudged the critical line separating "pro-abortion" from "pro-choice." Collapsing these two conceptual categories successfully slapped another label on the Democratic candidate, which did him a great deal of harm among middle-of-the-road Republican voters who may have been at least marginally dissatisfied with the performance turned in by their own party during the preceding eight years. The Republican ploy was to equate "pro-choice" with "pro-abortion," and then to equate "abortion" with "murder." By muddying up Dukakis's stand on abortion and by collapsing the difference between decisions made and methods of decision-making, Bush's people successfully forestalled the potential defection of the dissatisfied conservative element. They had to do this in order to neutralize Dukakis's main sales pitch—his skill at handling public money—which is a traditionally Republican selling point.

Those who know Michael Dukakis suspect that in his heart of hearts, Dukakis could not, personally, condone abortion as an alternative to non-life-threatening unwanted pregnancy. But he was unwilling to make that kind of choice for any one else. Dukakis, unlike Bush, did not portray himself as the moral shepherd of his political flock; he modelled himself after the traffic cop on the corner, giving every one who goes by an even chance to get to wherever they decide their final destination should be. George Bush, on the other hand, declared by word and by action that he was ready and willing to make moral choices for the rest of us. His stand on abortion was particularly important because, like his stand on drugs, it gave away the fact that he did not appear to grasp the distinction between private principles and public policies. "Father Knows Best" was the hidden theme in George Bush's 1988 campaign rhetoric—as it is the organizing principle behind the fundamentalist Christian groups who pushed the Reagan-Bush team into accepting Dan Quayle as a negotiated compromise between the mainstream Republican Party and the expanding extremist bloc (National Public Radio broadcast 1988).

Klapp (1964), LaPierre (1954), Weber (1968), Harris (1987), Shils (Glass-man and Swatos 1986), and Janowitz (1966) have all noted that a paternalistic leadership style seems to be the political image of choice among economically beleaguered and culturally battered populations, such as those of post-Weimar Germany and—Harris would claim—post-industrial America. Both Reagan's and Bush's patriarchal leadership style was not lost on the voting public, suggested by respondents in the 1988 survey who assigned to George Bush those "presidential" traits most closely aligned with privileged, charismatic leaders.

By contrast, in his dogged emphasis on the right of every individual to make his or her own moral choices, in his commitment to social programs which would yield a truly educated electorate, even in his somewhat Madisonian selection of Lloyd Bentsen, a sort of political alter ego, as his running mate, Dukakis epitomized the post-Enlightenment version of a democratic leader. His unwillingness to thrust government into the moral realm was consistent with the signature ideas of the U.S. governing documents, in which protection against the "tyranny of the majority" (Madison 1953) was so conspicuously a concern. But in his fraternal approach to wooing the American electorate, Dukakis may have credited them with a higher level of political sophistication than was realistic. In some respects, Dukakis was a philosophical throwback, an Enlightenment-era man trying to persuade Gesellshaft society people to seize control over their own lives and to make their own moral and political decisions. That takes energy. More energy, perhaps, and more belief that the individual person can and does make a difference in the political life of the nation, than our alienated, disillusioned, economically fretted electorate can currently muster up.

Many factors conspired to keep Michael Dukakis's various charms out of public view, and many of these "factors" can be attributed directly to media manipulation of the symbolic environment in which the 1988 election took place. More unsettling than the results of this single election—which was, after all, only one among many—is the implication that the American people may *want* to be manipulated, that they may, of their own free will, cling to the symbols of a nation which, in rational assessment, no longer exists. Most problematic of all is the possibility that a profound shift in American social attitudes may be underway. From this last suspicion, the most appalling question of all emerges. Are American voters, in the closing decades of the century, as eager to surrender their moral autonomy as were German voters in the 1930s? And, if so, to whom are they surrendering, and what are the terms of the deal?

In the original design of the American system of government, God was never intended to have the vote. But lest any one hasten to write off the influence of organized religion in this new era, the Bush-Reagan-Quayle era of American politics, remember that fully one-third of the delegates at the 1980 Republican convention were self-described "born-again Christian fundamentalists" (Conway and Siegelman 1982, 282), and that, in 1988, plans to run religious reactionary

Pat Robertson for president in 1992 were already under way. In 1988, the average annual income of delegates at this convention hovered around $60,000 each (Conway and Siegelman 1982). Born-again money is out there, and the born-again voice in the American political arena is not going away. If the 1988 election results and the rabid fundamentalist presence in the 1992 presidential campaign are any indication, demands from the religious right will only become louder and more uncompromising as time goes on.

As we tie together the patterns of moral and political philosophy explicated in this chapter, questions remain as to whether apprehensions about the ascension of the religious right in American politics are historically unfounded anxieties. In addressing this issue, we come full circle, returning to theories about the role played by the mass media in the formation of public opinion.

It was Harold Lasswell who first formulated what he called the "bolshevik" model of political propagandizing later seized upon by American fundamentalist groups. In his article "The Strategy of Soviet Propaganda" (Conway and Siegelman 1982), Lasswell identified three distinct stages through which propagandizing groups must pass on their way to political domination.

The first of these steps is the creation of "primary nuclei," as Lasswell terms the hard inner core of extremist political movements. This dedicated cadre must be capable of expansion; its primary purpose is to drive an opening wedge in the body politic. Often this initial assault enlists the aid organized youth groups, such as the Young Nazis in Hitler's Germany or the Young Bolsheviks in early Soviet Russia. Parallels in the American religious right might include the Teen Breakfast Club, the Young Christian Fellowship, and similar organizations.

Once the young and fervent are organized, the next step is to use them as a means of gaining national attention, while at the same time cooperating with allies in those arenas of power accessible to the "nuclei," who are by this time strong enough themselves to function on the level of "parties," "unions," and the like. We can find evidence of this happening in the growing numbers of young "born-agains," and in the puzzling fact that although, in 1988, Bush's credibility as an economic administrator was fairly low among the 18–34 segment of the population, 60 percent of the voters in this category, when polled, indicated that they would vote for the Bush-Reagan ticket (Church 1988, 28–30). Then, too, a substantial number of Pat Robertson's backers for the U.S. presidency fell into a youthful demographic niche. Robertson's drive for the White House was a far cannier political move than it may have appeared on the surface, for despite the long-shot odds of his success, the mere fact that he ran gave disparate fundamentalist groups around the country a reason to consolidate their political efforts. This aggregate constituency could then be brandished over the heads of the "mainstream" Republican war lords who sit behind the scenes and who make the back-room bargains—and who, in an election year, might be particularly sensitive to the perils of party fragmentation. Better to make a deal with the devil than to split the Republican vote.

The media play a vital role during this phase of Lasswell's model. Their contributions are two-fold. First, it is through the mass media that symbols of moral righteousness are created and subsequently wed to suggestions for political action. Second, it is only through the conduits provided by mass media channels that the illusion of a morally superior and ever-growing "majority" can be maintained—and may share one or two select concerns with the totally dedicated right (Conway and Siegelman 1982). A good example of this would be the remarkable and undoubtedly temporary liaison between feminists and "born agains" in the crusade against pornography. If the metaphor may be forgiven, more unlikely bedfellows than these could hardly be found. But, adhering to the strategies outlined in Lasswell's work, these two political out-groups, espousing profoundly antithetical philosophies of life and society, have, nonetheless, combined forces against a common enemy. Alliances are made which enlarge the sphere of influence which a political minority might rightfully expect to enjoy, and another step in the slow march toward center ground is achieved.

As the pornography example illustrates, the key to cementing these important temporary alliances, and, indeed to penetrating national consciousness itself, is the linking of specific political action with an abstract religious or philosophical belief. Weber (1947, 1958, 1968) pointed this out long ago, and Goebbels (Bramsted 1965) practiced it often in his much-publicized, intensely-studied development of Nazi propaganda strategies. History offers numerous examples of this principle in action. The insights of Jacques Ellul (1964, 1970), a French social philosopher, have particular significance for this analytical review of the American fundamentalist movement's possible political ambitions.

Truly effective propaganda must be total, maintains Ellul. It must happen on the national scale and it must happen at every level of community life and social experience. It must utilize all forms of the mass media, employing each one in a slightly different fashion to address a slightly different sector of the target population. And it must appear to "... reach for something higher, to appeal to some larger purpose, or, better yet, to the indisputable attraction of the mystical" (Conway and Siegelman 1982, 273). This mystification of material-world politics creates a sort of mythical ether, under cover of which political propaganda can go to work. Ellul and others (Conway and Siegelman 1982) argue that this creates a social environment in which the effects of propaganda can be most keenly felt by its selected targets:

> We are here in the presence of an organized myth that tries to take hold of the entire person. Through the myth it creates, propaganda imposes a range of intuitive knowledge, susceptible of only one interpretation, unique and one-sided, and precluding any divergence.

> This myth becomes so powerful that it invades every area of con-
> sciousness ... controls the whole of the individual, who becomes im-
> mune to any other influence. (272-73)

In their infiltration of American national politics, Conway and Siegelman (1982) go on to say, Christian fundamentalists display both a taste for and great talent at achieving precisely this kind of mythical saturation:

> The fundamentalist right model may be the most comprehensive of
> all, comprising the classic elements of total propaganda: a mam-
> moth mass communications network, a tightly coordinated political
> machine, a fiercely independent educational system—all predicat-
> ed, for the first time, on the deep structure of religion and suffused
> to grass-roots levels through a coalition of separatist churches, Bi-
> ble study groups, parachurch and missionary organizations.... Play-
> ing as it does on profound currents in religion and American
> history, the myth of the fundamentalist SuperChristian may be the
> most potent mythical image of modern time. Going beyond Aryan
> mythology and socialist abstraction, fundamentalist right supernat-
> uralism is uniquely compelling. It appeals, not only to the ancient
> religious images that continue to hold sway over most Americans,
> but to modern themes of morality and patriotism, to urge to surren-
> der in the face of overwhelming change and complexity, and to un-
> tapped spiritual and psychic potentials many Americans are
> reaching to explore. (276)

Although it's tempting to regard Conway and Siegelman's gloomy assessment of the religious right's hold on the American mind and soul as paranoid
hyperbole, the similarities between their conclusions and the separate findings of
Weber (1968), Harris (1987), Tonnies (Pappenheim 1959), and Lasswell (Conway and Siegelman 1982) are too striking to ignore. But if there is even a shred of
truth in what Conway and Siegelman propose, communication scholars and public policy designers need to begin looking at our systems of mass communication
with a far more critical eye than has historically been the case in American communications studies, examining their potential for deliberate and socially malignant misuse as well as their potential benefits as a nationally unifying
communications network.

The third and final step in Lasswell's tripartite model is the seizure of
political control by the propagandizing minority group. Conway and Siegelman
(1982) trace the infusion of religious leadership into the ranks of traditional conservatives, beginning with the formation of fundamentalist political action committees (PAC groups), think tanks, and lobbies in the early 1970s. They point to

the 1978 mid-term elections as an indication of early political rumblings, since a fair number of fundamentalists unseated Congressional mainstream incumbents at that time.

By 1979, they claim, "movement loyalists" had worked their way into key spots on important Senate committees, including the crucial Budget Committee, a strategy being replicated in the 1990s by the fundamentalist infiltration of local school boards. By the time Ronald Reagan arrived on the national scene in late 1979/early 1980, the internal crusade of arch-conservative Senator Jesse Helms and the fund-raising wizardry of the Moral Majority had set the stage for a quiet revolution in the halls of secular power.

Throughout his lengthy presidency, Reagan was careful to appear godly without seeming extravagantly "religious." His ties to the fundamentalist movement have remained in the murky background of his political record, although Conway and Siegleman (1982) claim that he was the darling of the religious right as long ago as 1969, when, as governor of California, he supported the California State Board of Education decision to teach creationism along with evolution in the public school system. But of greater interest than Reagan's past allegiances was his relationship with the American mass media, and what that may foreshadow regarding Presidents to come.

Many sources have commented on Reagan's unique and seemingly miraculous ability to use the media to further his own ends. From the very early days, when the "Teflon Man" myth was born, to the 1988 presidential campaign, during which the weakest link in the Republican forces—Dan Quayle—was efficiently hustled out of easy media reach, the relationship between the Reagan-Bush folks and the normally bloodthirsty mass media has been as puzzling as it has been cozy. The authors of *Holy Terror*, Conway and Siegelman (1982), have some ideas about why this might be the case.

> ... in his role as chief executive, Ronald Reagan is not using the nation's media solely for the purposes of public information ... in his first year in office, he repeatedly took advantage of his unique access to the media, mounting broad-based propaganda offensives which relied heavily on indirect means of manipulating public opinion, congressional legislation, and other integral functions of the democratic process.... the Reagan strategy combine[d], for the first time in an American President, the bold use of overt political propaganda carried out in unofficial cooperation with extra-governmental forces. Foremost among those forces is the vast propaganda network of the fundamentalist right, including leading elements of the electronic church and the new right's direct-mail, direct-phone, and other high-technology channels. (297–98)

Conway and Siegelman continue in this vein, charging the Reagan Administration with conspiring to install Christian fundamentalism as the reigning American *modus operandi*, with all that implies for the traditional freedoms of speech, thought, and multivariate worship. Regardless of the degree to which they are correct in their accusations of incest between U.S. religion and U.S. politics, Reagan's media magic is well-documented in many quarters, including both the scholarly and the popular press. Given the historical perspectives of Tonnies (Pappenheim 1959), Harris (1987), Weber (1958), and Bramsted (1965), and the work on leadership and public opinion done by Weber (1968), Lasswell (Conway and Siegelman 1982), Klapp (1964), and Lang and Lang (1966), it seems clear that the question is not *whether* the situation described by Conway and Siegelman is possible, but, rather, *what* the in-breeding of religious comfort and cultural anxiety might actually mean in terms of future American attitudes about the role of moral autonomy in the self-governing process.

Certainly it seems clear that, to some limited extent, at least, the political appropriation of cultural myth is, indeed, occurring within the arena of presidential elections. The degree and severity of this situation, and its implications for the future good health of representative self-government in this country remain uncertain. But the evidence suggests that the issue needs to be examined at length and in depth by communications scholars, politicians, media practitioners, and, perhaps most importantly, by the voting public, itself. It is to precisely this question that the political perception survey and the advertising panel analyses, described in the next two chapters, address themselves.

Chapter III

Competing Visions of an American President

Catalyzed by the curiosity of sociologist Gladys Lang and a group of research colleagues at the University of Washington, the rest of this book reports on a series of interlocking empirical projects, beginning with an account of a voter perception survey conducted in 1988. This survey, and the series of subsequent respondent interviews accompanying it, are discussed in this chapter.

The survey itself divides naturally into three related segments, identified as: 1) the closed, or structured, survey questions; 2) the voter open-ended survey questions; and 3) the follow-up interviews, which I conducted with approximately five percent of the survey respondents. A copy of the political perception survey form may be found at **Appendix A**. The analysis of data collected from the survey was processed using the Statistical Package for the Social Sciences (SPSS) computer program.

The sample

The sample consists of 97 Seattle-area high school students and 186 college undergraduates in the University of Washington's School of Communications, yielding a total of 283 test cases. Ages within the combined respondent pool ranged from 15 to 38 years; the high school students, specifically, fell between 15 and 20 years of age, whereas the college people were between 17 and 38 years old.

In terms of gender division, the high school sample contained an almost equal number of male and female students, with 48 male and 49 female respondents. The college group was weighted heavily with female participants, showing 122 women respondents compared to 64 males. This disproportionate gender distribution was controlled for during data analysis.

The psychographic attribute, "interest in politics," was reported as moderate for the high school sample, with 57.7 percent of those surveyed indicating their degree of interest falling between three and six on a ten-point scale, which defined "0" as being "not at all interested" and "10" as being "very interested". College-age respondents appeared to be somewhat more motivated politically, since 65.4 percent of them reported an interest level falling between five and eight on the same continuum.

Media exposure levels to pre-election coverage of the candidates and the campaign issues varied tremendously within high school/college categories, but overall the college-age respondents appeared to follow press coverage of the political issues more closely than did their younger counterparts, although it is unclear whether they were propelled to do so by personal interest or because their instructors required it of them.

One interesting side note to this survey research project involves the use of young people—college and high school students—as a sample population. Social scientists, traditionally, find themselves in the position of making use of "what's at hand"—typically, the undergraduates to whom they have access—as research subjects. In the case of *Stolen Thunder*, this phenomenon turned out to be something more than making a virtue out of necessity, since one of the primary research goals was to explore the ways in which new voters absorb socially constructed concepts about "reality," which may subsequently affect their perceptions within the political arena, and people in the high school age bracket are, almost by definition, "new" voters.

One case in point is the respondents' reactions to the word "reactionary," a menu item in the structured part of the questionnaire. Younger respondents tended to associate the word "reactionary" with left-wing politics, whereas older respondents attached to it right-wing connotations. Whether the credit for evolving notions of "reactionary" can be laid at the feet of the mass media is an interesting question, but the salient issue here is that, without "tapping into" the young voter crowd, the notion that the word itself may have acquired some new shades of meaning would never have surfaced. In that sense, capitalizing on the convenience of a captive student sample yielded unexpected dividends. Of course, the non-representativeness of student-based surveys is, as always, an impediment to generalizing from the survey findings.

The survey findings

Here's how the survey respondents reacted to the issues and the candidates in the 1988 presidential campaign. Except where otherwise indicated, the total number of possible responses for any given question is 283.

- **"What do you remember as the three main issues of the campaign?"**

Taxes (114 responses), addressing the *federal deficit* (106 responses), and *defense spending* (84) were cited as the three main issues of the campaign, followed by abortion (64), the nomination of Dan Quayle as a vice-presidential candidate (37), and foreign relations (29).

- **If you were the U.S. President and you could solve just one problem facing the country today, what problem would you choose?"**

Reducing the *federal deficit* (56 responses), solving the *homeless problem* (27), and waging a successful *war on drugs* (22) were cited as the three most salient problems facing hypothetical presidents at the time of the 1988 election.

- **"Which of the following traits do you think it is important for a U.S. President to have?"**

The results presented here (see Table 3.1) are rank-ordered according to the percentage of college-age respondents who selected each item, since the high school section of the sample did not provide usable responses to the question. The percentage of total respondents who selected that trait is indicated next to each item.

Table 3.1   Most Important Presidential Traits

Trait	Percentage
1. Open to new ideas	95.2
2. A good communicator	94.1
3. Competent	93.0
4. Experienced in foreign policy	89.6
5. Realistic	85.0
6. Honest	84.9
7. A good negotiator	80.0
8. Knowledgeable about history	74.2
9. Optimistic	70.8
10. Good with money matters	69.4
11. Inspirational	67.0
12. Flexible	57.5
13. Tough	48.1
14. Family oriented	42.2
15. Kind	30.8
16. A "Washington insider"	16.3
17. Firm religious beliefs	15.7
18. Male	12.5
19. Athletic	9.2
20. Good-looking	7.6
21. Young	4.9
22. Tall	4.3

Note: N=186 (College only)

Respondents were also asked to **rank-order the three most important traits for a U.S. President to have,** in descending order of importance. The three traits which were cited most frequently as being of primary, secondary, and tertiary importance were:

1. *competent* (28.1 percent of the respondents picked this for first place);
2. *a good communicator* (15.1 percent picked this for second place);
3. *open to new ideas* (15.2 percent picked this for third place).

Here's how the 1988 presidential candidates "stacked up" against the survey respondents' abstract image of an ideal president. The members of the survey sample were asked to assign any of 21 descriptive terms, also called "menu items," to either, or both, of the two candidates, as they saw fit. Here are the rank-orderings of items which people actually chose to assign to one candidate or another.

• **The three descriptors most often selected for George Bush were:**
   1. conservative (91.1);
   2. presidential (64.0);
   3. silk stocking (63.6).

• **The three descriptors most often selected for Michael Dukakis were:**
   1. liberal (96.5);
   2. hard-headed (43.4);
   3. arrogant (40.4).

• **The three descriptors selected least often for George Bush were:**
   1. *liberal* (3.5);
   2. *honest* (20.9);
   3. equal levels of response for the traits *boring, trustworthy,* and *vigorous* (27.5).

• **The three descriptors least often selected for Michael Dukakis were:**
   1. *privileged* (3.6);
   2. *presidential* (9.6);
   3. *All-American* (10.6).

- **The three most widely perceived shared traits were:**
  1. *patriotic* (60.1);
  2. *competent* (57.9);
  3. *intellectual* (59.6).

It's interesting to note that both candidates scored poorly on some of the survey items. For example, one of George Bush's lowest ranked scores was "honest," since only 20.9 percent of respondents who picked "honest" for either candidate picked it for Bush. But of the people who completed the survey questionnaire, 40.9 percent thought that neither Bush nor Dukakis was particularly honest; they left that menu item entirely unchecked. Thus, the percentage scores listed for both candidates reflects not the total percent of college respondents, but rather the percent of the total percent who actually responded to that particular trait on the behalf of either candidate. In other words, of the people who picked "honest" as any kind of presidential trait, 20.9 percent assigned that trait to George Bush; he was not described as "honest" by 20.9 percent of the total number of respondents.

Some traits won high scores, which were actually split between Bush and Dukakis. For the purposes of this analysis, a "high" score is defined as one which was picked by at 50 percent or better of the respondents.

The gap between respondents' perceptions of George Bush and Michael Dukakis, on an item-by-item basis, follows in Table 3.2. Again, only the college sample supplied usable answers to these questions.

Table 3.2 Traits Attributed to 1988 Presidential Candidates

Trait	Bush Score	Dukakis Score	Percentage Difference
Competent	27.1	15.0	12.1
Boring	27.5	40.2	12.7
Honest	20.9	36.4	15.5
Shrewd	50.0	32.5	17.5
Patriotic	31.2	8.7	22.5
Well-organized	43.9	13.8	30.1
Silk-stocking	63.6	27.3	36.3
All-American	57.5	10.5	47.0
Presidential	64.0	9.6	54.4
Privileged	59.1	3.6	55.5
Conservative	91.1	3.2	87.9
Liberal	3.5	96.5	93.0

Note: N=186 (College only)

Of particular interest was the way in which younger voters defined the constituent elements of "liberal" and "conservative" ideology. When asked to indicate whether they considered a particular "character trait" to be either a "liberal" or a "conservative" quality, they identified and rank-ordered "liberal" and "conservative" traits, *per se*, as indicated in Table 3.3 and Table 3.4, respectively. In this case, only the college sample is used because the high school respondents were too young to qualify as voters, "new" or otherwise.

It is particularly interesting that, in an almost perfect inverse relationship, the top three traits for conservatives were perceived as the bottom three traits for liberals.

Traits which came the closest to approaching parity between ideological poles, that is, those traits which were equally likely to be described as being both "liberal" or "conservative" characteristics, were dominated by the following respondent choices:

1.   *intellectual* (19.8 of the respondents said that this could be either a liberal or a conservative trait);
2.   *family values* (22.0);
3.   *patriotic* (32.8).

Table 3.3   Traits Perceived as Politically "Liberal"

"Liberal" traits	Percentage of respondent selection
1. Open-mindedness	92.9
2. Progressive	90.4
3. Personal freedom	90.4
4. Free speech	79.9
5. Reactionary	68.4
6. Using credit	54.5
7. Mainstream	33.9
8. Competitive markets	31.6
9. Intellectual	30.6
10. Family values	10.7
11. Strong defense	7.1
12. Elite	6.2
13. Patriotic	4.6
14. Traditional	3.8

Note: N=186 (College only)

Table 3.4   Traits Perceived as Politically "Conservative"

"Conservative" traits	Percentage of respondent selection
1. Traditional	93.0
2. Strong defense	90.3
3. Elite	88.4
4. Family values	67.3
5. Mainstream	63.7
6. Patriotic	62.6
7. Competitive markets	62.3
8. Intellectual	49.6
9. Using credit	37.5
10. Reactionary	25.4
11. Free speech	11.0
12. Progressive	7.4
13. Personal freedom	7.1
14. Open-mindedness	5.2

Note: N=186 (College only)

When asked whom they would cast as the leading man in each of the candidate's hypothetical film biography, respondents replied with a wide variety of choices. The most frequently cited actors for each of the two candidates were:

George Bush:
> 1. *Ronald Reagan* (15 responses)
> 2. *Robert Redford* (9 responses)
> 3. *Gregory Peck* (6 responses)

Michael Dukakis:
> 1. *Dustin Hoffman* (40 responses)
> 2. *Jon Lovitz* (9 responses)
> 3. *Danny DeVito* (7 responses)

(N=283)

Comparisons by gender

Three traits, in particular, seemed to vary greatly in their relative appeal to men and to women, within the limited confines of this research. "Tough" was the most conspicuous gender-linked variable. Males picked "tough" as a desirable presidential trait at a rate of almost two-to-one (54.1 percent compared to 26.5 percent) over females. Conversely, almost a third more females than males cited "optimistic" as an important presidential trait; the percentages for this menu item worked out at: females, 71.9 percent and males, 55.9 percent. "Athletic" as a desirable presidential trait also evoked a distinct difference in reaction between the sexes, with the selection rate registering at 18 percent for men and only 7.6 percent for women.

Seemingly superficial personal traits, such as "tall," "young," and "good-looking," appeared to have more appeal for male than for female respondents. Although the actual percentage differences for selection of these traits was very small, the relationship between the differences was startling. For example, only 9.9 percent of the men who answered the questionnaire indicated that a president should be young, a finding not too remarkable in its own right, until one compares it with the female response to the same trait, which was only 4.7 percent. Although only a small fraction of the male respondents indicated that youth was an important presidential attribute, that small fraction was still almost twice as great a response rate as the female reaction to the same item.

Similar patterns emerge for several other traits. Again, although the percentages involved are very low, more than twice as many men as women felt that a president should be tall (8.2 percent compared to 3.5 percent). Almost twice as many men as women felt that a president should be good-looking (11.7 percent compared to 5.9 percent). Male preference for a male president was also suggested, with the male respondents stating, at a rate of about two-to-one over females, that a president should be male (11.7 percent vs. 5.9 percent).

Two traits which women selected more frequently than did men were "honest" and "kind," although not by a large margin in either case, (87.1 percent to 83.8 percent for "honest"; 34.5 percent to 27.9 percent for "kind").

Although gender differences did surface from the cross-tabulations, many traits did seem to appeal almost equally to male and female respondents. In particular, of the people who responded, men and women seemed to agree that a president needs to have good communication skills, flexibility, a sense of family values, a realistic approach toward life, financial ability, negotiating talents, and the ability to inspire others.

Table 3.5 provides percentage responses by gender to the "desirable presidential traits" menu presented in question #14 on the political perceptions survey questionnaire. Again, although the sample numbers are low, the results evidence a striking pattern of gender affinity for contrasting bundles of character traits seen as necessary for a U.S. president to possess.

Table 3.5   Trait Selection by Respondents' Sex

Trait	% Male	% Female
Tough	64.9	36.1
Experienced in foreign policy	96.4	85.8
Tall	8.2	3.5
Competent	80.2	86.0
Young	9.9	4.7
Honest	83.8	87.1
Kind	27.9	34.5
Good communicator	93.7	94.7
Firm religious beliefs	19.8	13.5
Knowledgeable about history	72.3	76.0
Good-looking	11.7	5.9
"Washington insider"	18.0	12.9
Flexible	65.3	53.2
Athletic	18.0	7.6
Inspirational	65.8	62.6
Good with money matters	74.1	73.7
Realistic	85.6	87.7
Family-oriented	42.3	40.4
Good negotiator	77.5	79.5
Optimistic	55.9	71.9
Open to new ideas	92.0	97.1
Male	11.7	5.9

(N=283)

Summary of survey results

Several intriguing relationships among data are noticeable immediately. Foremost among these is the apparent contradiction between what the respondents said they wanted in a president, and what they perceived as desirable traits in a presidential candidate.

Presidents, indicated the respondents, need to be competent, open-minded and good communicators. "Liberals," presidential or otherwise, were seen as conforming to this general description—as being open-minded, progressive, and deeply involved in protecting personal freedom. "Conservatives," on the other hand, were perceived as being more removed from the needs and the access of the "everyday person"—as being traditional members of the national elite, concerned primarily with maintaining a strong defense; they scored, as a group, dramatically low in terms of being open-minded and in protecting free speech and individual freedoms. But George Bush, whom 91.1 percent of the respondents saw as being "conservative," was also seen (by 64.0 percent) as being "presidential." Michael Dukakis, who was perceived by only 9.6 percent of the respondents as "presidential" material, was nonetheless seen by 96.5 percent of this same group as being "liberal"—which, by the respondents' own definition, contained two of the three most important traits that a president should possess. This response pattern doesn't seem to have a lot of surface validity—in syllogistic terms, it could be described as A equals B; B equals C; but A *doesn't* equal C. There seems to be an internal paradox happening in how American see the president and how they perceive traditionally polarized liberal/conservative ideologies.

One explanation may be that the difference between presidential image and presidential reality shakes out in the ideological no-man's land between contemporary public perceptions of "liberal" and "conservative." Although people expected "good" presidents to *act* like liberals (in terms of defending human rights like freedom of expression and individual liberty) they wanted them to *project* the elitist imagery associated with political conservatism. Even bearing in mind very small numbers and a non-representative sample, it's still intriguing that, once the concepts of "liberal," "conservative," and "presidential" are put under a microscope, it seems that what people expect of the political categories themselves contradicts what those people expect of the candidates who fit—or don't fit—into those "liberal" or "conservative" categories.

The notion of the president's need to be a "good communicator," as indicated by a second-place finish in the presidential traits rank-ordering list (94.1 percent) and by its reappearance as the second-place finisher in question #15, may or may not be a legacy from the Reagan era, during which the press corps repeatedly affixed that title on the chief executive.

Although the three traits on which Dukakis scored most poorly converge in deadly combination—"privileged," "presidential," and "all-American," it's interesting to note that respondents, nonetheless, distinguished between "patriotic" and "all-American" in their assessments of the candidates. The percentage difference between Bush's and Dukakis' scores for "All-American" was 47 percent, yet only 22.5 percent of the respondents thought that Bush was more "patriotic" than Dukakis. The repeated link between "privileged" and "presidential" in the inverse high-low scoring for each man is also intriguing, since it may suggest that despite populist rhetoric, Americans may prefer to draw their leaders from the upper classes, a notion which the Bush strategists may have exploited on both sides of the electoral coin.

During the course of the campaign, Bush repeatedly downplayed his privileged background—particularly his education at Yale University. But although the Republican strategy was to keep Bush talking about his self-made manhood in the Texas oil fields, the visual imagery surrounding Bush and his family was a relentless portrayal of wealth and privilege—gamboling on the White House lawns, eating lobster at the family estate in Maine, heading the table at huge "Dallas" style barbecues, and so on. Bush's words about himself said one thing; pictures about Bush said another. Perhaps the two sets of information registered with the public in different ways. As Marsha Kinder (1984) and others have noted, the manner in which human beings process visual information differs from that in which they absorb written or spoken material—material coded in language instead of in pictures. Visual information, Kinder (1984) suggests, lodges on the visceral level, as opposed to print information, which worms its way into human perception through the far less primal means supplied by linguistic cognitive processes. Perhaps this would allow competing messages, such as those surrounding Bush's elitist background, to be accepted simultaneously, since the conflicting information is stored, so to speak, on different shelves in the public mind.

Follow-up interviews

Each interview lasted between fifteen minutes and half an hour. The sessions were conducted in the radio news lab facilities of the University of Washington's School of Communications, located on the Seattle campus, and were tape recorded using standard audio tape cassettes or 1/4" reel-to-reel equipment, as available. Written notes also were made, and general impressions of the interview sessions were abstracted from those notes at the end of each interviewing segment. A standardized interview data collection instrument was developed in order to maximize consistency of the information-gathering process during these sessions.

Respondents for the follow-up interviews were selected according to several criteria, one of which was their willingness to be interviewed. Of greater research interest, but perhaps less practical importance, was their degree of political conviction, as expressed in the survey responses. People from both extremes of the political spectrum were the ones who most intriguing, but, unfortunately, few of these people volunteered to be interviewed. Of all those who did volunteer, the great majority described themselves as "liberals" or "near-liberals."

A total of seven people were interviewed. The ages of these six women and one man ranged from 19 to 24 years, for an average age of 20 years. The apparent weighting toward female interviewees was unintentional; despite repeated attempts to solicit male interview subjects from among those who took the survey and indicated their willingness to be interviewed, only one male ever showed up for the interview session, although three others had been scheduled to participate.

Four of the seven interviewees had voted in the Bush-Dukakis election (three for Dukakis, one for Bush), which they indicated on their survey forms was not necessarily consistent with their parents' voting behavior. On a one-to-ten scale of political interest, with "0" indicating "no interest" and "10" indicating "very interested," they averaged a score of 4.6.

Similarly low-to-moderate scores were found for their media exposure index, as measured on the survey instrument. The survey question addressing the degree of media exposure sustained by each participant allowed for 24 separate sub-exposures, or "media events," such as "first presidential debate" "second presidential debate," "election returns," and so on. As a group, the interview subjects, on the average, took part in 15.7 of a possible 24 such events. Further data suggests that they didn't really talk about the election or the campaign issues very much, either; their responses on the survey form indicated, on the whole, a moderate amount of pre-election discourse with family, with friends, and in classes.

Respondents felt that the 1988 election had been preceded by a particularly "dirty" campaign, citing television as a contributing factor to this unsavory brand of political decision-making. Two commented that elections were always unpleasant experiences, one way or another. For many, this was the first presidential election in which they were eligible to vote; even these, however, referred to earlier campaigns as having been, in some way, "better."

Four respondents were extremely unhappy with the role played by the media in the 1988 race, fingering the political advertisements as conspicuously unfortunate instances of media intrusion into the political arena. People described the ads as "rotten," "a low blow," and "disgusting." The general feeling seemed to be that the ads lowered the general integrity level of the campaign. One woman condemned the ads vigorously, but then cited a Dukakis ad (the spot in which the candidate, closeted with his advisers, discusses Bush's untrustworthiness as a national leader) as a reason for making her decision to vote for Dukakis rather than for Bush.

The televised debates fared rather better. Overall, people felt that they got more information about the candidates from the debates than from the news coverage of the campaign or from the advertisements. Several people expressed dissatisfaction with the questions asked of the candidates, and several felt that the candidates "slid around the topics" and didn't really commit themselves to anything specific during the debate sessions.

When asked if they felt like they had a "real choice" between candidates, most of the respondents seemed to feel slightly dissatisfied with both Bush and Dukakis as potential American presidents, but only one tied the media's involvement in the primaries to the "viability" of the eventual party selections. It seemed to be a pretty close choice for most of the respondents. Many said that they felt Dukakis and Bush were drastically different on an issue-by-issue basis, yet when asked this generalized question about choice, they expressed the seemingly contradictory belief that there wasn't much significant difference between the two men. One respondent mentioned that, "It didn't matter which party you belonged to, as long as you were rich." Another young woman made the somewhat startling and historically inaccurate comment that "There have never been any rich Democratic presidents."

When asked if they thought that the election process was working (with the follow-up question: If so, does the media help or hurt this process?), a number of respondents replied with very different answers. One pointed out that although she felt the system worked well overall, the electoral college had outlived its usefulness and now did nothing more than discourage people from voting, since it weighted results in favor of certain states over others. Computers could be used to keep track of individual votes, she went on to explain, thus eliminating the operational need for the electoral college system.

Responses to the question about media intrusion into politics varied widely. Several people responded with, "debatable," or some similar remark, going on to elaborate their answers in different ways. One person felt that Dan Quayle probably would not have been a suitable candidate in pre-television days, since he "got in" mainly on his looks and "charm." By way of contrast, other people cited Quayle as an example of the way in which the media can victimize candidates unfairly, placing the vice-presidential candidate in uneasy company with Gary Hart.

Two people said that the media were helpful in bringing out public issues, but that they didn't do very much to let the public know what the candidates really intended to do about those issues. In other words, the media may have their uses as an agenda-setting device, but they fall short as a source of real information about the agenda which they help to define. Several people said that the public was just too busy to pay attention to the media—and to the candidates—like they should. Respondents seemed to be unclear as to whether or not this job of information clarification and gathering should then, by default, fall on the shoulders of the media.

One person said that the most accurate thing about the electoral process was the high degree of non-voting, which he seemed to feel was an accurate reflection of how people felt about politics. "Yes," he responded, "it (the voting process) is recording the wishes of the nation accurately because we have turned into a country of apathetic people."

Responses to the word "reactionary," by and large, indicated that people don't really know what it means. Several respondents came right out and said that. Those who did attempt a definition tended to lump it with "liberal" as a political concept. "Left-wing," "beyond liberal," "revolutionary," and "politically active—like in the '60s" were some of the terms used here.

Impressions of the words "liberal" and "conservative" indicated, overall, that "liberal" was perceived as somehow being the more deviant political attitude. Even people who described themselves as "liberals" seemed to feel that the word had extremist connotations, as if they were, for some reason, an ashamed minority. Several people said that "liberalism" was in some way related to the 1960s, when, they went on to imply, things were "pretty out of control." The general feeling was that "liberal" implied change, something new, whereas "conservative" implied stability, preserving what was "normal."

One woman spoke at great length about these two words. Her feeling was that college-age people ("all my friends, at least") were embarrassed to vote Democratic; likewise, they would be embarrassed to describe themselves as liberals. Her reason for this was that they were all in pursuit of the "good life," which she described as being characterized by owning cars and "condos" and other consumer goods, going on to say that aligning oneself with the Democratic Party ran counter to all of these things. "Poor people are Democrats," she said, "and we don't want to come across as poor people, so why should we vote Democrat?" She went on to say that if, by some fluke, a rich person acted like a Democrat, it meant that there had to be something wrong with them; they were somehow suspicious because they wanted to "give away" all of their money and social advantage. This respondent was a motivated, articulate young woman who had voted for Dukakis and who described herself as a liberal. She noted that her parents were both Democrats, but had been out of the country when the election ran and so couldn't vote. When they got back to the States, she called them. "I voted for Dukakis," she said. They congratulated her. "Thank you," she said. "I did what I thought was the right thing to do." Pause. "But don't tell anybody, okay?" (Paraphrased from notes.)

Several people said that they felt the words themselves, "liberal" and "conservative," had been given new and specialized meanings within the course of the 1988 campaign, although they couldn't say for sure how those new meanings may have differed from previous interpretations. One person said that he thought lots of people made their voting decision based on just one issue, and that this issue tended to act as a kind of self-definition for whether or not a person saw himself as liberal or conservative. For example, a pro-choice person who also supported gun control might define himself as "conservative" based solely on his attitude toward firearms.

Most people cited the media's tendency to seize on telegenic issues as the reason behind the discrepancy between what they remembered as issues from the campaign and what they felt was really the major problem facing the country. The general feeling seemed to be that if some one looked good on television, they had a fair shot at being turned into a viable political candidate, regardless of their personal or professional qualifications for the job.

When asked about their selection of a leading man for the hypothetical movie roles of Bush and Dukakis, people tended to be rather vague in their responses. One young person said that he'd cast Ronald Reagan as George Bush not because he felt any sort of similarity between the two, but because Reagan could play any given role at any given time.

By and large, people hated the ads. They claimed to find no usable information in them whatsoever, although several respondents did contradict themselves at other points in the interview by citing information from the ads as reasons behind their eventual voting decision. The woman who cited Willie Horton as a member of Dukakis' campaign staff couldn't remember where she got that impression. People who answered incorrectly the survey question about which of the candidates had served in the Armed Forces blamed the media—and in one case, the Dukakis strategists—for giving a false impression of the situation. Several felt that the press did not "play up" Dukakis' Army service the way that they had emphasized Bush's stint as a naval aviator, to the eventual detriment of the Dukakis campaign.

In response to specific words and phrases in the multi-part questions, people felt that neither Bush nor Dukakis was truly "presidential," with the exception of one woman, who felt that Bush was, "on the surface," everything that a president should be—"tall, blond, slim, athletic, all-American looking"—despite the fact that she voted for Dukakis. One person said that Dukakis "looked foreign" and that this worked against him. Most of the respondents felt that it could be taken for granted that being a "good communicator" was a critical part of being a good president, although one person said that he felt the trait had been over-rated by the press (or the public). "It's important that he (a president) be able to communicate well with Congress, and with his staff," he said, "but how often does he really have to communicate with us—and when he does.... how many of those guys do you think ever write their own speeches, anyway?" (Paraphrased from notes.)

None of the people interviewed could really define, in concrete and consistent terms, what they meant, exactly, by the word "presidential." It was described, variously, as "a certain air people have," or "they way he carries himself," or "an attitude." The abstract concept "presidential" seemed to operate on a different, perhaps deeper level than language; criteria other than those which can be articulated by the rational mind seemed to be at work.

Conclusions from survey

In general, the seven people interviewed in this set of sessions seemed to be disillusioned with both the electoral process and the media's role in it. The general distrust level was high, even when the respondents couldn't fully articulate what it was that they distrusted. They all felt that the media were important within the election process, and most felt that they were also misleading in one form or another. Even Dukakis supporters seemed to feel that Bush was the more "attractive" candidate, in the sense that he was a more familiar, perhaps less complicated media product. People seemed to feel, by and large, that the media were more useful in raising issues than in discussing them—or in getting the candidates to discuss them—but also that, sometimes, the issues raised by the media and focused upon by the candidates were not the real concerns of the nation at large. Perhaps one of the most arresting comments was the remark that post-Reagan era young people tend think of "liberal" as a socially extreme position, one which has no political history prior to the chaotic 1960s, and that it may actually embarrass them to vote for a Democrat, even when their personal sympathies may be in alignment with that party's concerns and commitments.

Chapter IV

Something for Nothing:
Television, Myth, and Political Culture

Continuing to probe the strategies by which cultural material may be turned to political purposes, an analysis of the mythic elements contained in each of two long (28 minutes each) election-eve advertisements, aired during the 1988 presidential race, illustrates the remarkable utility of social anxiety as a tool of political persuasion.

The advertisements were viewed and analyzed on three consecutive days during the early part of April 1990. A focus group, or panel, of seven people, divided into three sub-groups, reviewed the lengthy presidential campaign advertisements, which aired the night preceding Election Day 1988. A copy of the research instrument designed for use in these analyses may be found at **Appendix C**.

Selected from University of Washington graduate students and their associates, respondents for the actual analyses were chosen according to criteria developed during the pre-test procedure, and were assessed using a specially designed "Respondent Political Profile" (RPP) form (see **Appendix B**). Panel analysts responded to what they saw in two ways: First, through a series of open-ended questions regarding the "American themes and values" which they perceived as being contained in each of the two ads; and, second, by "ticking off" items from a preselected menu, or list, of similar themes, the contents of which were based on material abstracted from the U.S. governing documents.

The focus group consisted of four men and three women, who represented a range of political attitudes and voting behaviors. To mitigate against a possible primacy effect in the tape presentation, tapes were shown to the respondent groups in alternating sequence, although, since there was an odd number of groups, two of them ended up seeing the Dukakis tape first. Technical difficulties with the video playback equipment forced the first sub-group to view the Dukakis tape on a much smaller screen than the one on which they had viewed the Bush tape. This may have negatively affected the overall impact of the Dukakis material, especially since the Bush tape was much more visual to begin with.

Organizing the data

The preliminary treatment of the data from the advertisement analyses looked for two types of responses. The initial concern was with the sheer amount of information gathered; in keeping with apprehensions about the potential intrusiveness of the research instrument itself, questions addressed in the preliminary data analysis included determining if: 1) the instrument unwittingly steered people into making certain responses to the ads, and 2) the instrument was sufficiently incisive to collect relevant information from a spectrum of politically oriented respondents.

Accordingly, the first step in the data analysis was to replicate the instrument evaluation procedure which was performed on the pre-test material. This was accomplished in three stages. First, a brief review of the pre-test responses revealed that a substantial amount of material had been elicited from each of the seven respondents. This suggested that the analytical instrument did, indeed, speak to the political sensibilities of respondents despite their varying positions on the ideological spectrum, since an instrument biased toward one side of the scale would be less likely to provoke meaningful reaction from those at the other political pole.

The number of menu items selected by each respondent for one candidate, but not the other, was then compared with the number of menu items that each respondent picked for both candidates. As with the pre-test, the fact that each respondent selected a respectable number of menu items unique to each candidate, as well as selecting a number of shared items, indicated that the instrument distinguished sufficiently between the two men, thus alleviating many fears regarding basic instrument design.

Structured responses

Results of the political advertisement structured analyses reinforced findings from the 1988 political perception survey in several important ways. Three general patterns emerged from the structured responses to these ads. First, the Bush ad elicited, overall, the selection of significantly more menu items than did the Dukakis spot. Second, no negative menu items were selected for Bush under the "leadership styles" category, even by Dukakis supporters. Third, menu items selected for Bush clustered around two central themes, repeated over and over again in the respondent choices: 1) America is the leader of the free world, and 2) Bush "has what it takes" to be president.

Responses to the Dukakis ad seemed to be far more intellectual than emotional, in marked differentiation from the reaction to the Bush material. There was also a conspicuously higher rate of agreement among participants reacting to Bush than to Dukakis. For example, from among the total responses regarding the three most frequently chosen personal themes for Bush, six themes had been chosen for him by fully 100 percent of the focus group members, regardless of their own, personal political inclinations. In contrast, there were *no* unanimous selections for the Dukakis ad. His top three themes (or "menu items") drew responses from six (84 percent), five (70 percent), and four (56 percent) people.

It should be noted that these responses rates are measured against a 100 percent rate involving a total of seven people, since that's how many took part in the ad analysis. Each group member, or respondent, would then represent about 14 percent of the total sample. A menu item which was selected by six people, for example, would be scored at approximately 84 percent of the total respondent vote.

There was a difference in the *type* of theme picked for each candidate as well as in the *rate* of consensus with which they were picked. Salient themes from the Bush ad centered around America's dominant role in the world community, the sense of "destiny" with which people credited Bush, and the economic and social opportunities traditionally associated with the United States. Prominent themes in the Dukakis ad were more cerebral, focusing on ideals concerning government.

Results of a simplified frequency distribution for the menu items dealing with American themes and values are presented in Table 4.1 and Table 4.2.

Table 4.1   What Respondents Saw in the Bush Advertisement

Rank order	Cultural theme	Percent of respondents citing this item
1	All true patriots wish to serve their country.	100
1	Democracy is the best form of government for everyone.	100
1	America is the guardian of world democracy	100
1	America is a land of endless opportunity	100
1	Things just keep getting better.	100
1	America is #1.	100

N = 7

Table 4.2   What Respondents Saw in the Dukakis Advertisement

Rank order	Cultural theme	Percent of respondents citing this item
1	We are all in this together	84
2	The strong must protect the weak.	70
3	People should have a 'say' in making laws that affect them.	56

N = 7

Respondents were also asked to indicate personality traits which they found desirable in a president, drawing from the same source list as had been provided earlier to the survey respondents. Of 33 possible choices in this section, four traits were selected unanimously for George Bush. All of the respondents indicated that Bush presented himself in his ad as a kind, sensitive, patriotic family man who was, in some essential fashion, a "champion." Michael Dukakis' ad, on the other hand, triggered a much less cohesive reaction, garnering a response from five (70 percent), five (70 percent), and four people (56 percent) for the traits "honest," "family man," and "defender of the weak," respectively. Apart from the one shared trait of "family man," the leadership myths into which each man tried to plug himself looked very different. Personality traits which the ad analysis panel respondents cited as the most conspicuous descriptors of the two candidates, based on their respective advertisements, are as found in Table 4.3 and in Table 4.4.

Table 4.3   Most Frequently Cited Traits for Bush

Rank order	Trait	Percent or respondents citing this item
1	a champion	100
1	a family man	100
1	kind/sensitive	100
1	patriotic	100
2	a warrior	84
3	destined to be president	70
3	a father figure	70
3	all-American	70

N = 7

Table 4.4 Most Frequently Cited Traits for Dukakis

Rank order	Trait	Percent or respondents citing this item
1	honest	70
2	a family man	70
3	a defender of the weak	56
3	open to new ideas	56

N = 7

The only theme in which Dukakis "outperformed" Bush by a margin of 50 percent or better was item #39, "the strong must protect the weak," which pulled in responses from five people (70 percent), compared to a zero response rate for Bush. With regard to the differences in their personal leadership styles, this pattern continued. Bush "beat" Dukakis 7–1, 6–0, and 5–0 on the items "champion," "warrior," and "all-American," respectively.

There were some interesting gender distinctions among the respondents' reactions to the tapes. Despite the problems traditionally associated with subjecting minute samples to cross-tabulation analysis, the information yielded by this interpretation is intriguing, despite its minimal statistical usefulness.

Comparing item selection with gender for the Bush advertisement, it is somewhat startling to find that several menu items were selected exclusively by the men in the focus group panel. In contrast, there were *no* items for Bush selected only by women.

Four of the men, but none of the women, cited George Bush as "tall, self-reliant, a good communicator, and larger than life." Other gender-favored traits and themes for the Bush ad are presented in Table 4.5 and in Table 4.6.

For the purposes of this analysis, the word "frequently" has been defined to mean that an item had been selected by between 75 percent and 100 percent of the total number of people—divided by gender—who participated in the analysis.)

Only one menu item—#42, "a defender of the weak"—was selected for Dukakis by 100 percent of the male respondents. Many items for Dukakis were selected only by men, but they were selected only by one or two men for each item.

Two items, "self-reliant" and "good-looking," were selected for Dukakis by three (75 percent) of the men and none of the women who participated in the analysis.

Table 4.5   Items that Men Cited Frequently for Bush
(got 75–100% of total male vote)

Item #	Item description
3	God is a higher power than earthly government.
9	All true patriots wish to serve their country.
1	America is the guardian of world democracy.
14	Democracy is the best form of government for everyone.
21	God is on the side of the right and just.
22	Progress is a wonderful thing.
26	There are no problems we cannot solve.
27	Where there's a will, there's a way.
30	If you work hard enough, you'll succeed.
32	Peace through strength.
34	America is a land of endless opportunity.
38	People are basically good.
41	a champion
49	a man destined to be president
53	a family man
54	a father figure
60	self-reliant
62	a good communicator
65	kind/sensitive
67	all-American
68	a good negotiator
69	patriotic
70	competent
72	stable
73	decisive

N = 4

The only menu item for Dukakis to be selected by all of the women in the study was item #64—"open to new ideas." Three other Dukakis tape items to be selected by women and not by men were the leadership traits "team player" (358), "realistic" (63), and the theme "It's not whether you win or lose, it's how you play the game" (#31). It must be noted, however, that these female-only traits were based on feeble frequency levels; each received only one vote from the women involved in the analysis.

Table 4.6   Items that Women Cited Frequently for Bush
(got 75–100% of total female vote)

Item #	Item description
7	The state should protect freedom of religion..
9	All true patriots wish to serve their country.
12	Hard work and honesty will make you rich.
13	America is the guardian of world democracy.
14	Democracy is the best form of government for everyone.
21	God is on the side of the right and just.
26	There are no problems we cannot solve.
27	Where there's a will, there's a way.
30	If you work hard enough, you'll succeed.
32	Peace through strength.
34	America is a land of endless opportunity.
35	Things just keep getting better.
37	America is No. 1.
41	a champion
50	a self-made man
53	a family man
54	a father figure
59	a warrior
61	honest
65	kind/sensitive
67	all-American
69	patriotic
72	stable

$N = 4$

Unstructured responses

A massive volume of information generated in response to the open-ended questions contained on the ad panel analysis instrument. Analysis began with a thorough reading of the unstructured responses, comparing their content against the results of the subsequent structured analysis for each case. By and large, information contained in the unstructured section fell into the three related categories, which were suggested to the respondents at the time of the viewings: themes about the candidate, themes about the (campaign) issues, and themes about America.

Following this first step, the contents of the two parts were against each other, case by case, to make sure that respondent attitudes had not been affected by the presentation of a pre-selected menu of potentially presidential traits during the structured part of the analysis. More specifically, the unstructured material was reviewed in search of patterns of response regarding each of the two candidates and to determine the most frequently cited themes for the candidates, the issues, and the nation, and for remarks made by the respondents which might have added texture and depth to the necessarily terse responses given during the structured analysis.

Since the calculation of meaningful parametric statistics requires a much larger and more random sample than the seven people who comprised the focus group, statistical treatment was confined to simple percentages and frequency distributions, which organized data according to the following patterns and trends.

1. Most commonly cited general themes among:
   a. conservatives;
   b. liberals;
   c. moderates;
   d. males;
   e. females;
   f. overall.

2. Most commonly cited themes for Bush.
3. Most commonly cited themes for Dukakis.
4. Most commonly cited "presidential traits":
   a. by conservatives;
   b. by liberals;
   c. by moderates;
   d. by men;
   e. by women;
   f. overall;
   g. for Bush;
   h. for Dukakis.

5. Least commonly cited themes.
6. Least commonly cited "presidential traits":
   a. for Bush;
   b. for Dukakis.

7. Most commonly cited actor chosen to play:
   a. Bush;
   b. Dukakis.

Material provided by the respondents, which was elicited through the open-ended questions, reinforced that collected via the structured responses. Although a wide range of political affiliation and media consumption patterns was present among the ad analysis panel members, all of the respondents commented on *both* the content of the ads—picking out resonant mythic themes and cultural values—and on the technical presentation of that material, as a separate and important thing in its own right.

Dukakis supporters admired the technical excellence of the Bush advertisement—even as they bemoaned the "pedantic" delivery style of their own candidate's material. The most important cultural finding, however, relates to the sense of "destiny" with which the Bush ad was deliberately invested, and which provoked reaction from viewers regardless of their political sympathies.

Since the open-ended answers are as individualistic as they are comprehensive, no attempt has been made to condense them. Each respondent is identified only by the respondent code number, attached to the head of the file.

Liberal respondents (#006 and #011):

#006—As had been suggested in the directions, this person divided her reaction into three columns, headed "candidate," "campaign issues," and "United States," a *post hoc* system for organizing the open-ended information borrowed for use with the other respondent answers. Most of her observations about Bush fell into the "candidate" column (20 citations), followed by "United States" with 15 citations and then by "issues" with ten citations. This particular analysis was quite sophisticated, in that the respondent commented on the media techniques involved in producing the ads as well as on the content of the ads themselves. For example, under "issues" she listed "prayer in schools" and "pledge of allegiance," but then identified them as being media-generated "pseudo issues." Similarly, in the "United States" column she wrote "video shows happy, mostly white men," and later commented that "... the music is sickening when (Bush's) daughter is praising him." Clearly, the link between persuasive intent and technical execution was not lost on this respondent. Despite her many negative comments about Bush, however (six extended criticisms), most of her remarks in the "United States" category reveal positive imagery—eight of her fifteen entries report seeing "upbeat" images of American life contained in the Bush ad.

Her response to the Dukakis material followed a somewhat different pattern. Immediately noticeable was the inversion in sheer number of observations noted between the "candidate" and the "issues" column. Whereas the Bush ad had the most observations listed in the "candidate" and the "U.S." columns, the Dukakis ad, for this respondent, provoked only three notations in the "U.S." column and six in the "candidate" column. Dukakis' "issues" column, on the other hand, contained 21 notations. Although this person described herself as a liberal, four of the six observations made about the Democratic candidate were negative in tone ("seems to be on the defensive"; "trumpet bit was stupid"). The three "United States" observations were fairly generic and not tied to any specific visual imagery.

The well-stocked Dukakis "issues" column for this respondent was impressively comprehensive, reading like a referendum of social concerns: crime, citizen safety, drugs, the environment, education, Social Security, aid to small farmers, abortion issues, homelessness, affordable housing, and so on. This respondent also added a new item to the themes and American values section on the structured response form, writing in "... people have a right to be safe."

#011—This respondent, also categorized as a "liberal," saw the Dukakis tape first and the Bush tape second, in reverse order from #006. His reaction to the material, however, followed much the same pattern, in that the bulk of his citations for the Bush tape fell into the "nation" and "candidate" categories (30 for the "candidate" and seven for the "United States"), whereas his observation for the Dukakis tape revolved largely around "issues."

Despite this person's politically liberal orientation, many of the images he reported seeing about Bush were positive ones ("experienced, handsome, trustworthy, sweet, achiever, benevolent, honest"). He did have four negative comments about Bush, and, like the previous respondent, noted that the happy people in the Bush video were, by and large, white. His comments in the "issues" column for Bush were terse—"competitive, military, prosperity, religion"—as were his remarks in the "nation" column for Bush ("public service, spirit of democracy, freedom, strong world power").

Respondent #011's impression of the Dukakis material was conspicuously future-oriented; of the nine notations he made in this category, six used or were the word "future." He listed 14 items under the "issues" heading for Dukakis, identifying many of the same topics as did Respondent #006 ("crime, the environment, education, world peace, abortion"). Entries under the "candidate" column totaled 20 items, ten of which were negative toward Dukakis ("slimy, defensive, more defensive, boring"). Two penciled-in observations were interesting for their seeming contradiction: "not a feeling of strength" and "looking out for the little guy."

Conservative respondents (#008 and #014):

#014—This female respondent watched the Bush tape first and the Dukakis tape second. For Bush, she noted nine items in the "candidate" column, three items in the "issues" column, and four in the "nation" column. All of her observations regarding the candidate were positive—actually, all of her remarks within all three categories for the Bush tape were positive. She included in her written comments that this tape presented "nothing negative of the candidate." Specific notations under the column headings are here presented in their entirety, since they are so linked to the visual themes of the tape that it didn't make sense to summarize them separately. They also illustrate well the densely mythic texture of the Bush advertisement.

"Candidate" column remarks:
- upbeat ... always smiling; never seems tired
- strength—bigger/taller than Gorbachev in foreground
- patriotic—footage of war service
- heroic—tells story of battle.
- down to earth—black and white photos of him with his family, in work clothes; cooking; began "poor" in a one-room house
- courage—in light of the threat on his life
- compassionate—hugging elderly woman, boy, hungry child
- sensitive—choked up when given (deceased) police officer's badge.

"Issues" column remarks:
- peace/war—message not of arms control but that STRENGTH builds peace
- makes prayer in schools seem like an innocent, joyful practice with images of children waving at the camera as if to tell us they want to pray/let them pray.
- Peace through strength; after all, he fought in a war so he should know.

"Nation" column remarks:
- REBIRTH—child in '80s vs. war in the past—images of productive workers
- American Dream myth—flags, victories, war footage, smiling people, "we're the most wonderful country."

She listed six items in the "candidate" column for Dukakis, all of which were negative in tone ("cornball, a victim, on the defensive," and so on). Under the "issues" heading for Dukakis, she wrote four comments, one of which lists social concerns very similar to those mentioned by her fellow analysts (homelessness, crime, elderly, pro-choice, etc.). She also included in this section a remark about Dukakis's uncertain strategy in employing a question-and-answer format for his key political advertisement: "His voters aren't sure of him; they have questions."

Under the "nation" heading for the Dukakis tape, her two entries are "things are not great" and "the best America still needs to be built; it is yet to come." In closing, she writes of the Dukakis ad that: "The commercial is dull, too long on Dukakis, not enough fast editing. Facts, too many facts. Dukakis isn't having fun, he's preaching, he's lecturing us. Boring graphics, no music; not slick—concentration on the issues."

#008—Beginning his analysis with the Bush advertisement, this conservative respondent listed an almost equal number of observations among the three headings—22 for "candidate," 15 for "issues," and 17 for "nation." His comments on the candidate were largely complimentary ("financial Savior, compassionate but driven man, strong, identification with working man, philosopher, ready to fulfill his destiny, family man"), as were his remarks regarding the national image ("U.S. leading the world in civil rights, land of opportunity, America the greatest, God bless America," and so on). Unlike the other respondents, he also reported seeing messages regarding a variety of specific political issues in the Bush ad, including "drugs, law and order, taxation, unemployment, world peace." He also commented favorably on Barbara Bush's contribution to the candidate's image, citing her literacy drive under the "issues" column heading.

In his unstructured responses to the Dukakis material, he had 20 citations in the "candidate" category, 21 in the "issues" category, and 13 in the "nation" category. Six of his notations about the candidate Dukakis were negative in tone ("stiff, rigid, mystery man, defensive"). He, like several other respondents, identified Dukakis as being "on the side of the little guy."

His notations on the issues seen in the Dukakis tape were extensive and explicit, citing among the others "crime, campaign tactics, environment, strong military, strong economy, homelessness, cost of housing." He noted a perceived division between the interests of the rich and those of the lower and middle classes.

The national themes he took from the Dukakis ad included six negative items, among them "crime problems everywhere, country falling behind sociologically, country is economically weak, farmers under siege, a country of concerned, disillusioned people." He changed his final comment on the unstructured analysis, crossing out "America getting better" and writing in "America will get better."

Moderate respondents (#001, #010, and #007):

#001—This respondent wrote almost three times as many notations for the "candidate" column as he did for the "nation" column on the Dukakis tape analysis, which was the first tape he addressed. His answers differed in format from those of his colleagues in that he didn't adhere strictly to the three-column structure, presenting his remarks in a more narrative form.

The gist of his comments regarding Dukakis seemed to be that the candidate "came off" as "phony." He didn't like the question-and-answer format of the Dukakis program, noting that "... if I had seen this before the election, I think I might have voted for Bush."

Also, his criticisms of the "issues" presented in the Dukakis tape differed qualitatively from the other respondents' in his sophisticated approach to the rhetoric involved. For example, he states that Dukakis "simplified" the Social Security issue and quoted a statistic on the homeless that he felt was "suspect." Overall, this respondent supplied three negative comments on the candidate, four critical comments on the "issues," one neutral comment on the "nation" and two negative comments on the Dukakis advertisement itself.

His response to the Bush advertisement was more mixed. He noted a lack of issues-oriented content in the Bush ad, and cited what he felt were "propagandistic" plays on emotion, such as the "torpedo pilot" story. Among the things that he thought worked well in the Bush ad were the segments featuring testimonials by Barbara Bush, the "family sequence," the conclusion, during which Bush addresses the audience directly, and the generally "slicker" production values than those displayed in the Dukakis tape.

#010—This person generated an amazing amount of material in his response to the unstructured part of the analysis. After watching the Dukakis tape, which he saw first, he wrote 38 comments, 23 of which were negative in tone. Among these were the observations: "too analytical; too detached; I wouldn't like him; his own worst enemy; doesn't get to the point; bad format; needs to raise his voice; words, words, WORDS!" Two other comments command special attention. The respondent noted that, when Dukakis responded to Bush's personal attacks, he (the respondent) was disappointed because he wanted "a fight, not analysis" from Dukakis. And, in a puzzling but seemingly profound aside, the respondent remarked that Dukakis' shirt-sleeves "were a lie"—implying perhaps, that the candidate was not as "blue collar" as his image tried to convey.

Under the "issues" column, #010 listed many of the same topics cited by other respondents—crime, environment, Social Security, and so on. Several interesting additions crop up here; the respondent notes that "Dukakis might be right on the issues, but I can't stand to listen to him." He also cites "emotions of Dukakis" and "class conflict" as two problematic elements in the presentation of Dukakis' image.

Two of his comments under the "nation" heading question the use of television ads in general within the election environment. His third comment in this category makes reference to Dukakis's use of the American flag as a symbol of "a nation working together for the common good."

His responses to the Bush material were similarly detailed. He listed 25 themes under the "candidate" heading, 18 of which were complimentary ("good guy, courage, some one to be proud of"). Among these were some personal assessments of character, such as, "I like him—he has his quirks, but I wouldn't hold it against him" and "(displays) shock and outrage appropriately."

In the "issues" category for Bush he listed 17 items, many of which echoed topics contained in the replies of his fellow respondents. Interestingly, he added "greatness" as a campaign issue. Under "nation" he cited 15 positive themes, including "strength works," "happy," and "Russians coming to us."

This particular respondent scattered a number of editorial comments throughout the margins of the structured analysis, many of which are particularly revealing. Of Bush, he wrote that although the candidate was not "a man of the people," he was a "good person," and that Bush was a "warrior if need be" with a "reservoir of self-reliance." He said that Bush was not "open to new ideas," because he "already knows what's right and wrong" and that he was "larger than life because he's served his country." Dukakis, he wrote, was "smaller than life."

In contrast, he observed Dukakis as a "crusader for human rights—sort of" and as a "philosopher of the worst sort." He called him "... a loner ... off in his library with his books" and as being more "Pollyanna-ish" than realistic. He also remarked that Dukakis was "too fair" and "not open to any thinking but his own, and is a poor negotiator because he doesn't really know how to listen."

#007—The female respondent in this case study watched the Dukakis tape first and the Bush tape second. As did several other participants, she commented negatively on the question-and-answer format of the Dukakis tape, describing it as "too jerky—too stop-and-go."

In her response to the perceived thematic content of the advertisement, she listed 18 items under the "candidate" column, 12 items under the "issues" column, and zero items under the "nation" column. Nine of her "candidate" replies were negative in tone ("people seem whiny; problems, downers, repetitive hand gestures"). She observed the symbolic importance of visual details, such as Dukakis' removing his suit jacket in an attempt to seem more casual. As was the case with everyone who brought it up, she found the trumpet-playing sequence contained in the second half of the Dukakis advertisement, during which the candidate joins in what appears to be a community talent show/music contest, both distasteful and unbelievable.

Her assessment of the "issues" content in the Dukakis tape was comprehensive, running the gamut from abortion to farmers to negative campaigning. Again, as was the case with several other people, she noticed a heavy reliance on the "future" theme in the Dukakis piece, although she placed it in the "issues" category rather than under "nation." In her concluding comments on the Dukakis piece, she stressed the strategic error of emphasizing "the downer—the negative side ... problems, problems, PROBLEMS. No upbeat America break."

Her response to the Bush advertisement was very different. Under the "nation" heading—for which she listed nothing at all in response to the Dukakis ad—she noted nine items, four of which were positive ("world peace, world freedom, common sense; we're GREAT!"). Only two "issues," the prison furlough program and Dan Quayle, were listed, but 15 themes were provided in the George Bush "candidate" category—seven of which were positive ("winner, good nature, getting the job done" and so on).

Her summary comments for the Bush advertisement were cogent and insightful in their differentiation between the visual and the cognitive material contained in the ads. She wrote: "clear messages, well-presented. The powerful images of success made me proud; I feel good about the message and the messenger.... Sometimes the visuals speak for themselves."

Conclusions from both sections of panel analyses

To sum up, it appears that the overarching conclusion to be drawn from the panel analyses is that the clear, simple messages contained in the Bush tape elicited clear, simple responses based in the affective realm—"gut reactions," as it were, to the familiar themes of American life and a traditional American vision of leadership. Both the unstructured and the structured responses point very clearly to a telescoping of the conceptual boundaries between the destiny of the nation and the destiny of candidate Bush. Even people who were not Bush supporters, and who thus would be less likely to inject into the tapes messages they might prefer to see there, perceived the same traits and themes as those who were self-described conservatives. And Dukakis supporters, who were not predisposed to approve of the mythic material contained in the Bush advertisement, nonetheless felt "good about America" after looking at his tape, testimony to the eloquence of the argument which is waged on the affective rather than on the intellectual level of awareness.

In contrast, those who produced the Dukakis tape presented their material along largely cerebral lines; the frame of reference for this ad is intellectual, not emotional. And despite their attempts to portray a warmer, more "human" Michael Dukakis (the red sweater, the unfortunate trumpet-playing sequence, the shirt-sleeves and the cozy library), the result came across more like a political science seminar than like an advertisement. The Dukakis people, it might be said, defined their communicative mission as the imparting of information; the Bush people defined theirs as a sales job.

Even the two different choices of program format ran parallel with the two contrasting philosophies which each man brought with him to the campaign trail. The Dukakis tape, with its awkward question-and-answer format, seemed amateurish, clumsy, sincere, and defensive. It also put the emphasis on talk, not on pictures. Bush's tape, on the other hand, was seamless. It flowed like a cross between a documentary production and a World War II entertainment film. The use of romantic V-Day archival footage at the outset of the tape was a very clever touch, for it established a sense of affinity between the story of the man, George Bush, and the story of America, fresh from simple victory in glorious battle, as both the man and the country came of age in the post-war years. It invited viewers to frame George Bush as both the symbol and the product of that cleaner, brighter time.

Dukakis's tape, on the other hand, was a candid but lumbering attempt to establish intellectual fellowship with the viewers. Viewer emotion was treated almost as an afterthought, and a somewhat embarrassing one, at that. It may have been an honest piece of work, but it did not adequately exploit the medium in which it was presented. And—as this study has indicated—the cardinal rule for any type of cultural politics with ambitions on the American mind, as accessed through the American television set, inevitably reduces to an "exploit or be exploited" scenario.

Chapter V

Cultural Implications of Research Findings

Results from the different parts of this research project interact with one another in some interesting ways, suggesting some important implications for communication studies, as a scholarly field, and for making improvements to the U.S. protocol surrounding presidential elections, as a cultural process.

Although the 1988 presidential election provides a useful backdrop against which to study the way in which cultural material evolves into political communication may seem to focus on the two candidates themselves, it's important to remember that the real focus of this work is not about the relative merits of George Bush and Michael Dukakis. Rather, it's about the cultural nature of political discourse. *Stolen Thunder* merely uses the leadership traits and the mythical themes which each of these two men attached to themselves—or had attached to them—during the course of the 1988 campaign as illustrations of the social machinery which creates political material within a cultural framework.

Dominating the survey results, for example, was the simple notion that George Bush, in some ill-defined fashion, was a "winner" and that Michael Dukakis was not. This, really, gets at the central question in the issue at hand: Precisely what does the American public think that being "a winner" actually means? In 1988, Bush was perceived as a "winner" in all the right places, such as country, family, corporate workplace. Furthermore, he was perceived as being a "winner" in the most conventional sense of the word: As the survey results and the interview subjects indicated, Bush was seen as being a "patriot," a "warrior," a "tough guy," a "sensitive human being" and a "devoted family man"—all at the same time.

Television provided the means by which these sometimes competing descriptions could be simultaneously accommodated in a single person. In putting together television campaign material, over and over again, Bush used pictures and Dukakis used words. But Bush's messages were put in simple terms, whereas Dukakis's campaign talk was an endless parade of complex and compound sentences describing complicated cultural conditions and social processes. As a result, the image of Dukakis which finally emerged from all this intellect was far less conceptually cohesive, more fundamentally ambivalent, than was the picture of George Bush.

This is, of course, ignoring the question of whether *either* televised self-portrait—Bush's or Dukakis'—was true-to-life. The key point is that Dukakis's strategy demanded that people think in order to understand him, as a man and as a candidate, whereas all the Bush campaign asked of people was that they feel good, about themselves, about their country, and about Bush himself. Dukakis asked them to *think*; Bush asked them to *feel*.

Despite Dukakis's lead in the public opinion polls during the early part of the campaign, it could be argued that Bush began the 1988 race several lengths ahead of the Governor in terms of national exposure, since Bush's public life as director of the Central Intelligence Agency (CIA) and as vice president in the Reagan administration easily overshadowed Dukakis's political achievements in Massachusetts state politics. Nonetheless, using simple words and powerful pictures—just as prescribed in the Goebbels strategy outlined earlier—Bush associated himself with almost every one of America's most cherished national images. And, again and importantly, he did this through a series of concrete visual images.

At various times throughout his lengthy, pre-election night advertisement, Bush presented himself as the veritable quintessence of the following core American mythical heros: a young naval aviator, splendid in victory, magnanimous in triumph; as an enterprising young "oil man," pulling himself up by his bootstraps on the American frontier; as a stately diplomat, canny, shrewd, power-dressed and polite; as the watchdog of national security; as the bouncing, energetic, loyal vice president; as a benevolent and remarkably fecund family patriarch, and, finally; as the *inevitable* choice for "leader of the free world," a man not grasping at personal ambition, but merely fulfilling the bright destiny which lay in wait for him all of these years. In fact, Walter Shapiro's post-election article in *Time* (1988d) begins with the notion that, with his presidential victory, George Bush's resume is—at last—complete.

But Michael Dukakis had only one image, only one "package," only one myth with which he courted the American public, and the great tragedy of his campaign is that he never came to realize there was no natural market in American mythology for what he had to sell. We do not have much of a tradition, in this country, of popular support for real political intellectuals, who, in the United States, often seem to be swimming upstream. There are a few notable exceptions, such as Adlai Stevenson (who didn't win), John Adams (who was very much disliked), Thomas Jefferson (who did win but who died embittered), and Abraham Lincoln (whose intellectualism may have been the tortured product of his unique and agonizing historical moment). But intellectualism was Michael Dukakis's whole "shtick." He was a cerebral creature, a "rational man," and his campaign was based on the assumption that other people were motivated by the same type of intellectual impulse. And it died on its feet.

One could argue that, with the possible exception of Woodrow Wilson and Herbert Hoover, America has frequently preferred "doers" to deep thinkers in the

Oval Office. One bit of evidence for this notion is the American habit of electing generals to office, and then trying to impose upon them the itchy mantle of civic administration.

As the research results presented in this book suggest, the traits we Americans prize most in our leaders and the values we hug most closely to our national heart revolve around the twin virtues of decision and commitment. In response to the subjunctive mode survey question on this score, for example, the clear majority of the actors selected to play George Bush were men who have made their film careers as cowboys, spies, soldiers, and cops. They are all granite-jawed, laconic, self-assured and self-reliant heroes who shoot first and agonize over the ethics of it later. To be fair, they do sometimes agonize before they shoot, and they do, sometimes, miss. But the shooting, itself, seems to be important.

Conversely, who was the overwhelming choice to play Michael Dukakis? Dustin Hoffman—the thinking person's actor, famous in no small part for his persistent tackling of dark, complex, highly internal roles. Given the choice between a tortured soul and a simple cowboy, the Americans who took part in this research, at least, seemed to reach for the saddle, regardless of their political ideology.

Similar patterns emerge in a comparison between the survey results and the advertisement analyses results surrounding specific campaign issues. The success of the Bush strategy is perhaps best captured in the remarks of a young woman who, in her follow-up interview after completing the 1988 survey form, confided that she was embarrassed to vote Democratic because Democrats were "poor people, blue-collar people, and bleeding-heart liberals who feel really guilty and who for some unknown reason want to give everything away" (paraphrased from notes).

Young people, she insisted, wanted to associate themselves with the "good things" of American life—and that meant, in terms of the concrete, visible world, nice cars, a good home, a boat, a videocassette recorder, maybe an "RV" ... the icons of material success. As a result, she concluded, young voters were automatically attracted to the perceived "party of success," the Republican Party, as typified by George Bush and as depicted in such striking visual terms in the Bush television advertisements. They wanted to associate themselves with an ideology in much the same way—and perhaps for much the reasons—as advertisers associate consumer products with specific "desirable lifestyles." In short, at least some of these young voters were affiliating themselves with the Republican Party not because of its social values, but because of its market appeal testimony to the hypnotic power of material success, in politics as well as in consumerism.

The Dukakis campaign wasn't about "success" of any description; it was about taking a long look at some hard facts and about rebuilding America based on the somber realization that there was more to revive than to celebrate. The Bush campaign never even admitted to the social concerns that provided central issues of discussion in the Dukakis platform—an eroding national economy, a sense of inferiority abroad, crushing poverty at home, unaffordable health care and education, escalating racial tension, and armies of transient people choking the urban streets. Bush's message was brilliant in its simplicity: America has always been, is now, and will continue to be the greatest nation on the face of this planet. We are the fortunate few and it is incumbent upon us to maintain our position as world leaders ... and George Bush is the inevitable man to lead us ever higher.

This whole idea of destiny, so integral a component in all good leadership myth, was orchestrated exquisitely by the Bush campaign leadership. In stark contrast to Bush's high romance, Michael Dukakis's repeated emphasis on competency and logic reduced his bid for the White House to a mere job application, rather than framing it as a do-or-die attempt at a spangled, glittering fate. It was for this sober sense of perspective, more than anything else perhaps, that the American people never really forgave Michael Dukakis, because his personal realism and stolid conviction that the presidency was first and foremost a serious affair stripped away the voting public's sense of high occasion. His matter-of-fact approach to the nation's highest public office brought the lofty symbolism of that position down to grubby earth, where it could be muddied, trampled upon, worn at the edges like anything else in routine life.

More than his supposed personal coldness or professional unsuitability, Michael Dukakis's refusal to implicate himself in the playing out of national fantasies doomed his bid for the presidency. He didn't buy and he wouldn't sell the right kind of political myth needed to grease the skids to the Oval Office. Michael Dukakis would not let Americans fool themselves, and as both history and literature have demonstrated repeatedly, we can forgive our leaders, our prophets and our lovers almost anything but the truth.

Just because Dukakis clung to cold-eyed fact does not necessarily mean that he would have made a great president. But his failure is interesting because the means by which he eliminated his chance of becoming president illustrates the awesome power still wielded by mythic symbols within the contemporary political arena. Consider once again the *Time* magazine poll (Church 1988) in which the same people who reported deteriorating personal finances under the Reagan realm also said they'd vote for Ronald Reagan again in the upcoming election, since he was a Republican and Republicans were "good with money." And look at the differences between what *people* responding to this research project's Political Perception Survey perceived as the nation's No. 1 problem versus what the 1988 *candidates* purveyed as the foremost national crisis (reducing the federal deficit and lowering taxes, respectively, two rather mutually exclusive goals). Or, compare the personal trait that survey respondents valued most highly in a president—openness to new ideas—with the trait which they assigned to George Bush as a predominant personal characteristic—conservatism.

Similarly telling contradictions arise when considering the campaign treatment of drug abuse and drug-related crime. Only 22 of 186 respondents to the 1988 survey questionnaire (11.8 percent) cited drugs as "America's #1 problem." Yet the candidates—especially George Bush—repeatedly stressed the need for a vigilant war on drugs as *the* priority item for the incoming chief executive. The strategic reasons for this are discussed at length elsewhere in this book. Let it suffice to say here that the campaign rhetoric and visual imagery surrounding the drug war punched the same unifying nationalistic buttons as would a more conventional conflict, like a war or a national disaster—it served to bring an alarmed and galvanized citizenry back "home" to rally around a strong, essentially paternalistic, leader.

To some degree, both candidates in the 1988 race re-framed the drug abuse issue as a new threat to national security, but Dukakis's solution emphasized education, whereas Bush's emphasized force. Dukakis said, "Teach kids about the horrors of drug addiction." Bush said, "Get tough on drugs; arrest casual users and execute drug king-pins." Once again, the Dukakis approach was predicated on basic assumptions regarding self-government which issue directly from American governing documents: Specifically, the notion that, given all the pertinent information and the freedom to debate it, individuals will make choices which best benefit both themselves and the society in which they dwell. In contrast, the Bush proposal for dealing with the drug problem was to simply control individual behavior by taking away choice through the application of state power. These two very different philosophies of government are consistent with the overall contrasting attitudes of the two men, and were reinforced by the perceptions of those men, as reported by respondents in both the political advertisement analyses and in the political perception survey.

The guiding questions which informs this last part of this project is whether cultural myth be transformed into political myth during the course of an American presidential election, and if so, what are the processes by which this may occur and what implications may this have for the process of self-government?

The research reported here, suggests that yes, this is so—that cultural myth can be transformed into political myth through the use of the mass media, particularly through the use of television. Over and over again, respondents in both the political advertisement analyses and in the political perception survey reported *politically* oriented responses to what was essentially *cultural* information—for example, the idea that the nuclear family is the appropriate social morpheme for "normal" human living systems, the notion that destiny plays or should play a major role in matters of human government, and even the ambiguous but highly intriguing distinction which they drew between the concepts "patriotic" and "all-American." Just the mere fact that respondents with wide-ranging political sensibilities identified in George Bush's advertisement 109 of a possible 280 potent cultural themes is testimony to the notion that cultural myth can be turned to political purposes, since in comparison, a total of only 47 thematic responses were identified for Michael Dukakis's advertisement.

Once thus transformed, can political myth effectively divert public attention away from real and serious national problems and toward a preoccupation with the myth itself? This is a more difficult question to answer conclusively. Certainly the work of Harris (1987) and Bramsted (1965) bears eloquent witness to the diversionary value of using the media to set cultural brush fires. Findings from the survey questionnaire segment of this research, suggesting that the priority which the public set on the drug war differed substantially from the level of crisis which the 1988 candidates assigned to it, add currency to the historical perspectives. But this may be one of the few cases in which "more research" is truly required, as opposed to be glibly prescribed, since another study, using a truly random sample and designed more longitudinally, could be conducted to correlate election-year versus non-election-year media coverage of the drug issue against public perceptions regarding the gravity of the drug problem. This more generalizable research might be able to provide media scholars and political scientists with a more comprehensive picture of the media's role in shaping public opinion—and of the potential for subsequent hijacking of the drug issue by political forces.

Do deeply ingrained cultural myths, central to the society's vision of self, yield more emotionally potent political myth than do less highly charged narratives and imagery? Maybe. Certainly the realization that the Bush advertisement successfully punched important cultural buttons for *all* of the interview respondents, irrespective of their political beliefs and inclinations, would suggest support for this idea.

The question arises, of course, of how to distinguish between "potent myths," like those which I have called a "sustaining myth of culture," and their punier cousins. I tried to address that dilemma by drawing the menu items for the panel analysis form directly from the actual texts through which the United States first defined itself as a nation and as a system of government distinct from all others—namely, the Declaration of Independence, the Constitution, the Bill of Rights, and the work of their spiritual forebears in the Enlightenment era, as they were Americanized by Thomas Paine (1987) in his derivative revolutionary pamphlet, "Common Sense." The simple fact that most of these documents are under glass at the National Archives speaks of their proximity to U.S. cultural heart, as does the fact that we, ourselves, are so enamored of the governing principles which they espouse that much of 20th century American foreign policy has been concentrated on "bringing democracy" to the rest of the globe.

But the vital question remains partially unanswered: How does one measure the relative strength of emotional impact carried by competing political myths? Presumably, by behavior—in the case of a presidential election, by voting. Although exit interviews were conducted with all of the political advertisement respondents, gathering a rough sense of the relative vehemence with which they responded to each of the eighty menu items, the link between affective reaction and actual voting behavior still remains insufficiently clear, especially once differences in respondent personality, social background, and mood are taken into account. Human behavior is too complicated to chase backward toward simple conclusions regarding human attitude, and that invitation to reductionism puts at risk more sophisticated understandings of human action.

Perhaps one imaginative way of addressing this methodological conundrum would be to set up an experimental situation, in which the visual content of each ad—the pictures which accompany the spoken information—is swapped, each one being dubbed onto the soundtrack of the rival piece. In other words, researchers could run Michael Dukakis's soundtrack under George Bush's visuals, and vice versa, making the necessary electronic alterations in candidate voice quality as they do so. One group of respondents could watch the real ads; the other could be exposed to the manipulated versions. Analyzing and comparing responses from the two groups might be a way of parsing out more precisely which visuals were the most powerful in overcoming the personal symbolic baggage carried by each respondent and about which the researcher can, otherwise, know very little.

But all of this deals with methodology, fascinating to researchers but of little interest to those outside of the university community. What practical bearing do the results of this research have on the way Americans elect their president? Relative to this particular point, several implications for public policy present themselves, regarding the ramifications for self-government which may emerge as the social function of presidential elections shifts from being a truly administrative task to having a more symbolic focus. The most immediately important aspect to this is, perhaps, its invisibility—the idea that this type of functional shift could and might occur unheralded and perhaps even unnoticed by the very people on whom it would exert the most profound effect—the American public. And herein lies the greatest danger.

Elections—presidential and otherwise—have always had their ritual dimension, but the evidence presented in *Stolen Thunder* suggests that the symbolic contribution of these events is now their dominant aspect. Ritualizing the high drama of presidential politics is, in its own right, perhaps, no bad thing. It may, in fact, be seen as a healthy cultural adaptation to life in a sprawling, impersonal, Gesellschaft society like the modern United States.

Human beings need ritual to organize and to punctuate life just as surely as they need food and drink to sustain it. In every time and in every place where people have dwelt together, ritual and ceremony have arisen, along with the myths which both explain and preserve the communal ordering of human existence. It may very well be that the American presidential election is a natural heir to other, earlier types of ritual spectacle; certainly the epic scale on which it occurs and the social distance maintained between the actors (the political leadership) and the audience (the public, both voting and non-voting) would support this theory. As Walter Lippmann (1966) has noted, as industrialization has continued to alter the face of American culture, the emotional distance between the leaders and the led has widened considerably. At the apex of the national democratic system are Congress and the president. The power base descends hierarchically from there, flattening out to a broad platform of voters, about half of whom may be signaling, by their consistent refusal to vote, a sense of alienation from or disenchantment with the political system as a whole (Hoffman 1989).

Perhaps for these people, eligible but inactive voters, presidential politics, with its caucuses and conventions, banners, bunting, and balloons, has become a kind of circus. Certainly the American media, feeding on the ritual hysteria of a national election while simultaneously tearing hungry chunks from the body politic, often refer to it as such. That national elections retain any semblance of dignity, any flavor of being an event of serious mythic dimensions, indicates that Klapper's (1960) rule of minimal effects could be applied to mass politics as well as to the mass media: People will use presidential politics, much as they use the media, in whatever way best suits their own emotional and social needs. And that, in turn, suggests that presidential politics itself has become a kind of medium, has evolved into a public forum through which the American electorate debates aloud, as it were, the relative appropriateness and the continued utility of its ever-evolving visions of self and of reality. Presidential politics, and presidential "players," have become a kind of surrogate dreamscape, a canvas against which we Americans can project symbolically the defining elements of our culture so that we may examine them more closely, turning them this way and that as we search for hidden flaws in the constituent parts of our national "self." They provide us with a way in which to make concrete the ethereal landscape of our internal world, so that we may then re-assess, re-evaluate, and perhaps re-embrace the cultural values which inform that world and the social construction of reality which defines it.

Certainly the decline in voter participation that this country has experienced during the last century and a half emphasizes the spectator, as opposed to the participatory, component of national elections. Nineteenth-century voter turnout statistics put our own feeble century to shame. Eighty-three percent of all eligible voters cast a ballot in the presidential election of 1876; indeed, the mean turnout for all elections in the period between 1840 and 1860 was 70.3 percent, with presidential contests pulling in a voter response ranging between 69 percent and 83 percent (Piven 1988, 29–30). In contrast, of the 178.1 million people eligible to vote in the 1988 presidential election, the contest explored in the pages of this book, only 66.6 percent registered to vote and only 57.4 percent actually cast a ballot (U.S. Department of Commerce 1990, 262). In fact, of the world's 24 democratic nations, the United States hovers around second from the bottom in terms of voter turnout, achieving on the average a 53 percent participation rate, compared to Belgium, Australia, Austria, and Sweden, which score rates of 95 percent, 94 percent, 92 percent, and 91 percent, respectively (Piven 1988, 5). This situation lends some credence to the notion that American politics has become somewhat of a spectator sport, yielding largely symbolic and ritualistic contributions to our national life.

The impending threat lies not in this ritualization itself, but rather in the determined denial of its role in American national life. By denying the symbolic nature of the choices we make, we limit our vision regarding other choices involving more concrete political action which may run counter to privileged symbolic perceptions. In other words, if we are using our presidential elections primarily as a vehicle by which to choose one set of dreams over another, we must take care not to confuse the selection of dreams with decisions about reality. Informed political choice must rely on sound evaluation of the facts as well as on ideals. Conflating the latent and the manifest function of presidential elections, it then follows, could threaten the viability of our entire system of self-government.

As a voting public, it is absolutely critical that we be aware of our own motives and our collective sub-agendas in the political sphere. In an industrialized, mass-mediated democracy, where public opinion exerts such a profound influence on affairs of state, the perception of fact carries as much, if not, in some cases, more clout as does actual fact itself. The two worlds—cultural and political—cannot, must not, be separated conceptually. To do so opens the door to grotesque oversimplification of our self-governing process and the egalitarian society which it seeks to create.

In today's democratic state, good intentions are not enough. Clarity of vision is also required of voters who would seek to guide their own destiny, collectively and as individuals. Knowledge without self-knowledge is not merely insufficient; it is dangerous, for it leads to decisions propelled solely by desire. But true clarity—clarity with a predictive component, which is wisdom—rests on two pillars, not one. The first of these is realism, the capacity to assess character, events, and conditions for what they truly are, without flinching in the face of failed social aspiration or folding under the pressure of ugly economic truths. Michael Dukakis tried to sell his presidency on this kind of realism. But he failed, in part because he emphasized realism at the expense of idealism. He failed to grasp the fact that people need their illusions and that the constructive way to work with those illusions is not to puncture or deflate them, but rather to incorporate them into one's realism as occasional moments of vision ... which is the second underpinning of wisdom. Illusions—ideals, in a more positive framing—can provide a critical sense of perspective, a resilient optimism that makes the daily grind of improving the real world more tolerable. Psychologists insist that one needs to feel "good about" oneself before any meaningful internal change can commence. George Bush grasped that simple fact of human nature and ran with it—ran all the way to the White House. The most telling data of all to emerge from my research, I suspect, came in an exit interview with one of the focus group respondents, a Dukakis campaign worker, at that, who more or less said that after watching the Dukakis ad, she felt burdened; she felt like she was facing a long, hard job "cleaning up" America. But, she added, after viewing the Bush advertisement she felt "just plain good."

There are some crucial lessons to be drawn from this candor. The first of these is the realization that people fasten onto the image of a president whose leadership style and whose perceived picture of the social system most closely approximates their personal visions of an ideal world. Often these visions are coded as cultural myth, or are couched in mythic terms, since myth supplies a convenient language through which to articulate heavily freighted symbolic representations of belief. Frustration in this attachment process can result in frustration with and ultimate rejection of candidates who do not permit this cultural-political transference to occur.

We need to examine more closely the idea that we, in the United States, may use our presidential elections not to select new leaders so much as to ritually reinforce the privileged myths of our culture. Political myth and political imagery which has been derived from cultural themes with the greatest mythic potency—for example, the classic "American success story," the perceived superiority of a democratic form of government, the notion of the United States as the guardian of world freedom, and a sense that the head of such a dominant player in the global arena must possess the traditional personal characteristics of the dominant culture's "ideal" American male—tend to be the most effective.

In terms of improving U.S. election protocol, some concrete steps can be taken to acknowledge this phenomenon, and, perhaps, to compensate for the conceptual conflation which it invites. Such measures might include: imposing strict limitations on the amount of money that each political party is allowed to spend on pre-election media advertising; requiring the mass media to withhold election-night announcements about electoral college scores until after the western states have finished voting; perhaps, eventually, doing away with the electoral college altogether; passing legislation which makes voting a mandatory part of citizenship in the United States; and, most importantly, confining presidential candidate debates to radio transmission rather than encouraging their broadcast over commercial television networks.

Several of these ideas warrant a moment of closer scrutiny. The first of these is the idea that we, through legislative action or constitutional amendment, should require the media to withhold announcements about electoral college scores until all polls have closed and all results have been tallied. The reason for this is simple, and speaks directly to the disenfranchisement of the western states through the disproportionate weighting which is the electoral college's perhaps most charming feature. Information about electoral college results has more of a chilling effect on subsequent voter turnout than does news about momentary trends in the popular vote, for the simple reason that western voters—and others, who are through virtue of personal schedule as well as political geography, delayed on their way to the polls—are acutely aware that winning the electoral college means taking the election. This discourages many people from casting their vote in the face of a media-hypothesized electoral college trend—despite the fact that, if enough of these late voters did go to the polls, "sure things" might be reversed and self-proclaimed political "mandates" might be mitigated by a more complete, and thus, presumably, a more accurate reflection of national opinion.

Getting rid of the electoral college itself is easier said than done, although mine is not the first voice, nor the most significant voice, to urge doing so. But let us take a lesson from the judicial system, in which *dicta* as well as case disposition plays a role in shaping future court decisions. If we are, collectively, unhappy with the electoral college, then let us continue registering the popular vote after the electoral outcome has been decided, and then use those figures to challenge, over time, the distorted representation accrued through electoral tallies.

One sure way to improve U.S. voter turnout would be to fine people who don't vote. Alarming though it may seem, there is some justice in this idea. Neglecting or refusing to vote is not exactly the same thing as not participating in the election event; since incumbents traditionally enjoy an advantage in election situations, not voting, in essence, supports the maintenance of their *status quo*. Voting must be conceptually redefined as being a responsibility, as much as a right, of democratic societies. Revenues collected from those who choose to neglect their commitment to the democratic process could be applied to lessening the national debt or to similarly civic concerns.

Perhaps the most realistic—and the most immediately viable—of these ideas, is the notion of limiting pre-election debates (and perhaps all paid-for political advertising) to radio. Television introduces to the political message environment far too many spectacularly affective elements; it provides too much opportunity for manipulation through purely symbolic appeals. Allowing the candidates to debate their positions and to pitch their ideas on national radio, instead of on national television, protects their First Amendment right of free speech and provides them with a national channel through which to exercise those rights, while at the same time setting some parameters around the outrageous cost of television campaigning—which, in its own right, often discourages third-party and alternative candidates from even entering the political race. Voters would still have critical access to information about the candidates and the issues, but they would be spared bombardment by the symbolically-charged emotional imagery for which television is so uniquely perfect a vehicle.

Concluding comments

These suggestions are not perfect solutions, nor are they foolproof as a means of providing damage control against the symbolic manipulation of the American voting public. But they are, at least, places to begin addressing the problem. And they speak directly to the central questions propelling this research—the notion of piecing together circumstances that might account for what could be perceived as a puzzling set of election results in November of 1988.

Granted, to some people—to the many people who voted for Bush, obviously—the results of the elections were not puzzling. They were gratifying. But the fact remains that George Bush did not win the 1988 election with an overwhelming popular vote, such as Ronald Reagan enjoyed when he captured the presidency in 1980. Bush may have swept the electoral college, but with its winner-take-all system, the electoral college is hardly representative of voter preference in terms of real numbers. This suggests that the political balance was tipped by another institutional force. The results reported here indicate that the mass media are that force.

Through manipulation of the symbolic environment, the mass media, or elements using the mass media, are able to generate the illusion that a minority segment of the population is actually at the forefront of a sweeping political trend. Once created, cultural symbols which populate the social environment tend to linger in the public mind, sometimes long after their relevance to material reality has faded. It just happened to be, in 1988, the conservative element in American politics which worked the television crowd. Any ideological group, given the right tools and enough money, could repeat the Republican hat trick in elections yet to come, as long as we continue to focus public attention on the *political aspects* those elections without educating ourselves about their *anthropological* function.

Regardless of the accuracy of Conway and Siegelman's (1982) claims regarding the intentions of the radical religious right to infiltrate national politics, it seems important that we, as a society, take steps to contain the influence that avowedly apolitical systems such as our mass media may exert on public thought and political decision-making. Until we can undertake enough empirically based research to determine what is really happening in the American political arena—and in the mind and heart and, yes, soul of the American voter—we have to institute stop-gap measures. If not those suggested here, then something very like them must be developed, or our system of self-government may collapse under the crushing weight of widespread social alienation and political atrophy. For one thing, glimpsed however imperfectly, is certain.

America is rusting from the inside out. Without taking structural steps, the brief voter rejuvenation seen in the 1992 Bush/Clinton/Perot race will continue to be the exception, not the rule, in U.S. political life. The corrosion began, as it always does, with economic misfortune, but it has been fueled by social conditions and political symbology that achieve great feats of political myth-making for a number of special-interest groups, among them the New Christian Right. A poll conducted by the American Broadcasting Corporation (ABC) and the *Washington Post* (described in an Associated Press article in October 1990) reported that 79 percent of all Americans think that America is "in serious trouble." Nine out of ten people polled in a similar study felt that most Americans could no longer afford to go to college, a particularly sinister index to the frailty of our national commitment to equal opportunity (Magner 1990). How many of the people who responded to this survey, reporting such desperate feelings about the state of the nation, had gone to the effort of voting in the last national election? The research reported in this book, and in others, suggests that many of them did not—with the exception of those who belonged to radical political groups (liberal *or* conservative) or who were members of active religious organizations.

And although there might be fewer of these people than there are of the silent, unhappy middle-grounders, the very fact that they are so very driven to make their voices heard lends to those voices unnatural strength and resonance. Ross Perot's unprecedented success as a third party candidate in the 1992 race also testifies to the dense voter population inhabiting this unhappy moderate zone.

Granted, the moment was ripe, in 1988, for exploitation by a shrewd, driven minority. But the New Right could never have accumulated its political power—or have assembled its tremendous financial clout—without the great bulk of the American people aiding and abetting their activities through passive non-interference. By indulging in a kind of political inertia, the American public may have served as an accessory to the systematic murder of its own civil liberties; in the worst-case scenario, the public may have unwittingly collaborated in its own political suicide. Certainly this is suggested by the present mood in the halls of power, on university campuses, and upon the increasingly narrow benches of the nation's judicial system, where Supreme Court decision is sometimes brandished in one hand and the Book of Revelations in the other.

But the solution is not as simple as either gloom-and-doomers or as Pollyanna-ish optimists might suggest. Human decision-making, of which political activity is but one manifestation, is an intricate and multi-variate phenomenon. But I believe that it is, in the final analysis, understandable. And that which can be understood can be bargained with.

It may not be too late, if we can only rouse ourselves to understand that not all of this country's true enemies are hooked on "crack," or speak a foreign language, or sport "unsaved" souls. The right to disagree among ourselves has always been our most cherished and our most inalienable American liberty. Let us exercise it now.

It is time that we stopped focusing solely on loud condemnations of our many "external" foes and on vestigial ideals with little grounding in contemporary social reality, and began paying some measure of attention to whispered plans that are, perhaps, being laid at home, in our own political house, drawn up under the mass-mediated cover of an approaching twilight. The greatest American myth of all, perhaps, is that it is without conscious or concerted effort, and on the strength of historical momentum alone, that the United States will enter the 21st century as a just, safe, and equitable place in which to live.

Works Consulted

Abrahams, Roger D. (1972). Folklore and literature as performance. *Journal of the Folklore Institute, 9,* 75–95.

Allis, Sam. (1988, October 24). Of myth and memory. *Time,* pp. 21–27.

Back on track. (1988, September 26). *Time,* p. 23.

Bagdikian, Ben. (1987). *Media monopoly.* (2nd ed.). Boston: Beacon Press.

Barthes, Roland. (1968). *Elements of semiology.* New York: Hill and Wang.

_____. (1972). *Mythologies.* New York: Hill and Wang.

_____. (1988). *The semiotic challenge.* New York: Hill and Wang.

Bateson, Gregory. (1973). Style, grace, and information in primitive art. In Anthony Forge (Ed.), *Primitive art and society,* (pp. 235–255). London: University of Oxford Press.

_____. (1982). *Studies in symbolism and cultural communication.* Lawrence, Kansas: University of Kansas Press.

Benedict, Ruth. (1934). *Patterns of culture.* Boston: Houghton Mifflin Company.

_____. (1959). Anthropologist at work: Writings of *Ruth Benedict.* Boston: Houghton Mifflin.

Bennett, W. Lance. (1975). *The political mind and the political environment.* Lexington, Massachusetts: Lexington Books.

_____. (1980). *Public opinion in American politics.* New York: Harcourt, Brace, Jonanovitch.

_____. (1980, Autumn). Myth, ritual, and political control. *Journal of Communication,* 167–179.

_____. (1983). *News: The politics of illusion.* New York: Longman.

Berelson, Bernard, & Janowitz, Morris (Eds.). (1966). *Reader in public opinion* (2nd ed.). New York: Free Press.

Berger, Peter L. (1969). *A rumor of angels: modern society and the rediscovery of the supernatural.* Garden City, New York: Anchor Books, Doubleday.

Berger, Peter L., & Luckmann, Thomas. (1967). *The social construction of reality: A treatise in the sociology of knowledge.* Garden City, New York: Anchor Books.

Boas, Franz. (1955). *Primitive art.* New York: Dover.

Bocock, Robert. (1974). *Ritual in industrialized society.* London: George Allen and Unwin, Ltd.

Boorstin, Daniel J. (1962). *The image: Or, what happened to the American dream.* New York: Athenaeum.

Bouissiac, Paul. (1976). *Circus and culture: A semiotic approach.* Bloomington: Indiana University Press.

Bramsted, Ernest K. (1965). *Goebbels and National Socialist Propaganda, 1925–1945.* Ann Arbor: Michigan State University Press.

Breen, Myles & Corcoran, Farrel. (1986). Myth, drama, fantasy theme, and ideology in mass media studies. In Brenda Dervin & Melvin J. Voight (Eds.), *Progress in Communication Sciences,* Vol. VII (pp. 195–223). Norwood, New Jersey: ABLEX Publishing Company.

Brown, James W. & others. (1974). *Narcotics knowledge and nonsense: Program disaster vs. a scientific model.* Cambridge, Massachusetts: Ballinger Publishing Company.

Burke, Kenneth. (1969). *A grammar of motives.* Berkeley: University of California Press.

_____. (1969). *A rhetoric of motives.* Berkeley: University of California Press.

Campbell, Joseph C. (1968). *The masks of God: Creative mythology.* New York: Viking Press.

_____. (1982). *The changing images of man.* Oxford: Pergamon Press.

_____. (1985). *Myths to live by.* London: Paladin.

_____. (1988). *Historical atlas of world mythology.* New York: Harper and Row.

_____. (1988). *The power of myth.* New York: Doubleday.

Carey, James. (1988). *Myth, media, and narrative: Television and the press.* Beverly Hills, CA: Sage Publications.

_____. (1989). *Communication as culture: Essays on media and society.* Boston: Unwin Hyman.

Carlson, Margaret. (1988, November 21). Issues that mattered. *Time,* p. 37.

Cassirer, Ernest. (1946). *Language and myth.* New York and London: Harper and Brothers.

_____. (1979). *Symbol, myth, and culture.* New Haven: Yale University Press.

Cheery news to start your day. (1990, October 17). (Associated press wire story.), *The Daily,* p. 2. Seattle, Washington: University of Washington.

Conway, Flo & Siegelman, Jim. (1982). *Holy terror: The Holy fundamentalist war on America's freedoms in religion, politics, and our private lives.* New York: Doubleday and Company.

Cooley, Charles H. (1966). The significance of communication. In Bernard Berelson & Morris Janowitz (Eds.), *Reader in public opinion.* (2nd ed.). (pp. 147–155). New York: Free Press.

Church, George J. (1988, October 10) Are you better off? *Time,* pp. 28–30.

Corcoran, Farrel. (1987). Television as ideological apparatus. In Horace Newcomb (Ed.), *Television: The critical view* (4th ed.). (pp. 533–552.) New York: Oxford University Press.

Democrats for Economic Recovery. (1988). Meet Michael Dukakis—the new Mussolini. Lyndon LaRouche for President campaign literature. Seattle, Washington: November.

Descartes, Rene. (1980). *Discourse on method and meditations on first philosophy.*(1st ed.). Indianapolis: Hackett Publishing Company.

Devereux, George. (1961). Art and mythology: A general theory. In Bert Kaplan (Ed.), *Studying personality cross-culturally* (pp. 361–403). Evanston, Illinois: Row-Peterson.

_____. (1984). Fantasy and symbol as dimensions of reality. In R. H. Hook (Ed.), *Fantasy and symbol: Studies in anthropological interpretation* (pp. 19–32). London: Academic Press.

Dorson, Richard Mercer. (1971). *American folklore and the historian.* Chicago: University of Chicago Press.

Drugs: War on pot and paraquat. (1988, July 15). *Time,* p. 37.

Durkheim, Emile. (1915). *The elementary forms of the religious life: A study in the sociology of religion.* (Joseph Ward Swain, Trans.). London: Allen.

_____. (1933). *Division of labour in society.* New York: Free Press.

Eldridge, J. E. T. (Ed.), (1970). *Max Weber: The interpretation of social reality.* London: Michael Joseph, Ltd.

Ellul, Jacques. (1964). *The technological society* (1st American ed.). New York: Knopf.

_____. (1965). *Propaganda: The formation of men's attitudes.* New York: Knopf.

_____. (1970). *Prayer and modern man.* New York: Seaburg Press.

Fermia J. V. (1981). *Gramsci's political thought.* Oxford: Clarendon Press.

Fernandez, James W. (1966, Fall). Principle of opposition and vitality in Fang aesthetics. *The Journal of Aesthetics and Art Criticism,* Vol. XXV, No. 1, 53–64.

Ficte, Johann Gottlieb. (1868). *The science of knowledge* (A.E. Kroeger, Trans.). Philadelphia: Lippincott.

_____. (1889). *The science of rights.* London: Tribune and Company.

Fiske, John & Hartley, John. (1987). Bardic television. In Horace Newcomb (Ed.), *Television: The critical view* (4th ed.). (pp. 600–612). New York: Oxford University Press.

Frazer, Sir James George. (1935). *The golden bough: Part VI: The scapegoat.* New York: Macmillan and Company.

Geertz, Clifford. (1973). *The interpretation of cultures.* New York: Basic Books.

_____. (1976). Art as a cultural system. *Modern Language Notes,* (91), 1473–1499.

Gerbner, George. (1977). *Mass media policies in changing cultures.* New York: Wiley.

_____. (1981). *Communications in the 21st century.* New York: Wiley.

Giddens, Anthony. (1974). *Positivism and sociology.* London: Heinemann.

_____. (1978). In Gaye Tuchman's *Making news: A study in the construction of reality.* New York: Free Press.

_____. (1979). *Central problems in social theory: Action, structure, and contradiction.* Berkeley: University of California Press.

_____. (1982). *Sociology: A brief but critical introduction.* New York: Harcourt, Brace, Jovanovich.

Gitlin, Todd. (1987). Prime time ideology: The hegemonic process in television entertainment. In Horace Newcomb's (Ed.). *Television: The critical view* (4th ed.). (pp. 507–532). New York: Oxford University Press.

Glassman, Ronald M. & Swatos, William H. (Eds.). (1986). *Charisma, history, and social structure.* Westport, Connecticut: Greenwood Press.

Goethals, Gregor T. (1981). *The TV ritual: Worship at the video alter.* Boston: Beacon Hill Press.

Gramsci, Antonio. (1988). *Gramsci's prison-letters: A select translation.* London: Zwan in association with the Edinburgh Review.

Greenberg, Laura. (1975). Art as a structural system: A study of Hopi pottery designs. *Studies in the Anthropology of Visual Communication,* 2(1), 33–50.

Greenhalgh, Michael & Megaw, Vincent. (Eds.). (1978). *Art in society: Studies in style, aesthetics, and culture.* London: Duckworth.

Grimes, Ronald R. (1982). *Beginnings in ritual studies.* Washington, D.C.: University Press of America.

Hamilton, Alexander. (1957). *Selections representing his life, his thought, and his style* (Ed. and intro. by Alys Bowen.). New York: Liberal Arts Press.

Hamsun, Knut. (1920). *Hunger.* New York: A.A. Knopf.

Hand, Learned. (1952). *The spirit of liberty.* New York: Knopf.

Harris, Marvin. (1978). *Cows, pigs, wars, and witches: The riddles of culture.* New York: Random House/Vintage Books.

_____. (1987). *Why nothing works: The anthropology of everyday life.* New York: Simon and Schuster (Touchstone Books).

Hegel, George Wilhelm Fried. (1974). *The essential writings.* New York: Harper and Row.

Hertsgaard, Mark. (1988). *On bended knee: The press and the Reagan presidency.* New York: Farra, Straus, and Giroux.

Hoffman, Mark S. (Ed.). (1989). *The world almanac, 1989,* p. 322. New York: Scripps-Howard.

Kaeppler, Adrienne. (1979). Melody, drone, and decoration: Underlying structures and surface manifestations in Tongan art and society. In Michael Greenhalgh & Vincent Megaw (Eds.), *Art in society: Studies in style, aesthetics, and culture* (pp. 261–274).

Kafka, Franz. (1973). *Shorter works.* London: Secker and Warburg.

Katz, Elihu, Blumler, Jay, & Gurevitch, Michael. (1974). The utilization of mass communication by the individual. In Elihu Katz & Jay Blumler (Eds.), *The uses of mass communication: Current perspectives in gratification research.* Beverly Hills: Sage Publications.

Kellner, Douglas. (1987). TV, ideology, and emancipatory popular culture. In Horace Newcomb (Ed.), *Television: The critical view* (4th ed.). (pp. 471–504). New York: Oxford University Press.

Kinder, Marsha. (1984, Autumn). Music television and the spectator: Television, ideology, and dream. *Film Quarterly,* 38,(1), 2–15.

Klapp, Orrin. (1964). *Symbolic leaders: Public dramas and public men.* Chicago: Aldine Publishing Company.

_____. (1972). *Heroes, villians, and fools: Refelections of the American character.* San Diego: Aegis Publishing Company.

Klapper, Joseph T. (1960). *The effects of mass communication.* Glencoe, Illinois: Free Press.

La Fountaine, Joan S. (1972). *The interpretation of ritual: Essays in honor of A. I. Richards.* London: Tavistock.

LaPierre, Richard T. (1954). *A theory of social control.* New York: McGraw-Hill.

Lang, Gladys Engel & Lang, Kurt. (1966). The mass media and voting. In Bernard Berelson & Morris Janowitz (Eds.), *Reader in public opinion* (2nd ed.). (pp. 455–472). New York: The Free Press.

Lang, Gladys Engel & Lang, Kurt. (1983). *The battle for public opinion: The president, the press, and the polls during Watergate.* New York: Columbia University Press.

Lasswell, Harold D. (1966). Nations and classes: The symbols of identification. In Bernard Berelson & Morris Janowitz (Eds.), *Reader in public opinion* (2nd ed.). (pp. 27–42). New York: The Free Press.

Leach, Edmund. (1976). *Culture and communication.* London: Cambridge University Press.

_____. (1973). Levels of communication and problems of taboo in the appreciation of primitive art. In Anthony Forge (Ed.), *Primitive art and society,* 221–234. London: Oxford University Press.

Levi-Strauss, Claude. (1966). *The savage mind.* London: Weidenfeld and Nicholson.

_____. (1976). *Structural anthropology.* New York: Basic Books.

_____. (1979). *Myth and meaning.* New York: Schocken Books.

Lewis, I. M. (1976). *Social anthropology in perspective.* New York: Penguin Books.

Lippmann, Walter. (1966). Stereotypes. In Bernard Berelson & Morris Janowitz (Eds.). *Reader in public opinion* (2nd ed.). (pp. 67–75). New York: Free Press.

Locke, John. (1960). *Locke and liberty: Selections from the work of John Locke* (Intro. and Ed. Massimo Salvadori). London: Pall Mall Press.

Luther, Martin. (1943). *A compendium of Luther's theology.* Philadelphia: Westminster Press.

_____. (1974). *Selected political writings.* Philadelphia: Fortress Press.

MacAloon, John J. (Ed.). (1984). *Rite, drama, spectacle: Rehearsals toward a theory of cultural performance.* Philadelphia: Institute for the Study of Human Issues.

Magner, Denise K. (1990, October 17). 9 in 10 Americans say people can't afford college. *Chronicle of Higher Education,* p. A2.

Malinowski, Bronislaw. (1925). *The meaning of meaning: A study of the influence of language upon thought and upon the science of symbolism.* New York: Harcourt, Brace, and Company.

_____. (1944). *Freedom and civilisation.* New York: Roy Publishers.

_____. (1954). *Magic, science, and religion.* Garden City, New York: Doubleday.

_____. (1971). *Myth in primitive psychology.* Westport, Connecticut: Negro Universities Press.

_____. (1971). *Sex, culture, and myth.* New York: Harcourt, Brace, and World.

Manning, Frank E. (1983). *The celebration of society: Perspectives on contemporary cultural performance.* Bowling Green, Ohio: Bowling Green University Popular Press.

Maquet, Jacques. (1979). *Introduction to aesthetic anthropology* (pp. 1–47). Reading, Massachusetts: Addison-Wesley Publishing Company.

Madison, James. (1953). *Complete Madison: His basic writings.* New York: Harper.

Marx, Karl. (1976). *The German ideology* (3rd Rev. ed.). Moscow: Progress Publishers.

McCombs, Maxwell & Shaw, Donald. (1972). The agenda-setting function of mass media. *Public Opinion Quarterly,* 36, 176–87.

Mill, John Stuart. (1975). *On liberty* (1st ed.). New York: Norton.

Milton, John. (1973). *Areopagitica.* Cambridge, England: Deighton, Bell, and Company.

Mitgang, Herbert. (1990, January 31). A speech writer recalls the White House years. *The New York Times,* p. B2.

National Public Radio broadcast (1988, October 12). Seattle, Washington: KUOW-FM.

Nietzsche, Friedrich Wilhelm. (1924–74). *The complete works of Friedrich Nietzsche* (3rd ed.). New York: Macmillan and Company.

Noonan, Peggy. (1990). *What I saw at the revolution: A political life in the Reagan era.* New York: Random House.

Ottenberg, Simon. (1972). Humorous masks and serious politics among Afikpo Ibo. In Douglas Fraser & Herbert M. Cole (Eds.), *African art and leadership* (pp. 99–121). Madison, Wisconsin: University of Wisconsin Press.

_____. (1982). Illusion, communication, and psychology in West African masquerades. *Ethos,* 10(2), 149–85.

Paine, Thomas. (1974). *The age of reason.* Seacaucus, New Jersey: Citadel Press.

_____. (1987). *Common sense, and other political writings.* New York: Macmillan.

Pappenheim, Fritz. (1959). *The alienation of modern man: An interpretation based on Marx and Tonnies.* New York: Monthly Review Press.

Parks, Robert E. (1966). Reflections on communication and culture. In Bernard Berelson & Morris Janowitz (Eds.), *Reader in public opinion* (2nd ed.). (pp. 167–177). New York: The Free Press.

Piven, Frances Fox. (1988). *Why Americans don't vote.* New York: Pantheon.

Plato. (1928–1961). Address to Gorgias. Vol. 5 (Trans. by W. R. M. Lamb & Ed. by W. Heinemann London). Cambridge, Massachusetts: Harvard University Press.

Propp, Vladimir. (1968). *The morphology of the folktale* (2nd ed.). Austin: University of Texas Press.

Riley, Michael. (1988, November 21). Anatomy of a disaster. *Time,* pp. 46–47.

Rousseau, John Jacques. (1953). The social contract & Emile: On education. Both in Romain Rolland & others (Eds.), *French thought in the eighteenth century.* London: Cassell.

Schechner, Richard. (1977). *Ritual, play, and performance.* New York: Seabury.

_____. (1985). *Between theatre and anthropology.* Philadelphia: University of Pennsylvania Press.

Shapiro, Walter. (1988a, July 25). The party's new soul. *Time,* pp. 17–19.

_____. (1988b, October 3). It's the year of the handlers. *Time,* pp. 18–25.

_____. (1988c, October 24). Bush scores a warm win. *Time,* pp. 18–20.

_____. (1988d, November 21). Lots of work to do. *Time,* pp. 24–25.

_____. (1989, September 18). Feeling low over old highs. *Time,* p. 104.

Shibutani, Tamotsu. (1961). *Society and personality: An interactionist approach to social psychology.* Englewood Cliffs, New Jersey: Prentice-Hall, Inc.

Shils, Edward. (1975). *Center and periphery: Essays in macrosociology.* Chicago: University of Chicago Press.

_____. (1978). *Art and social life.* Teaneck, New Jersey: Somerset House.

_____. (1978). *Culure and mass culture.* Teaneck, New Jersey: Somerset House.

Shilts, Randy. (1986). *And the band played on: Politics, people, and the AIDS epidemic.* New York: Penguin Books.

Silverstone, Roger. (1981). *The message of television: Myth and narrative in contemporary culture.* London: Heinemann Educational Books.

_____. (1984, October). Narrative strategies in television science—A case study. *Media, Culture, and Society,* Vol. 6(4), 337–410.

Simmel, Georg. (1950). *Sociology of Georg Simmel.* Glencoe, Illinois: Free Press.

_____. (1971). *On individuality and social forms: Selected writings.* Chicago: University of Chicago Press.

Simpson, Roger. (1987, Fall Term). In lecture, University of Washington, (CMU 419).

Sinclair, Andrew. (1964). *Era of excess: A social history of the Prohibition movement.* New York: Harper and Row.

Smith, Adam. (1948). *Adam Smith's moral and political philosophy.* New York: Hafner Publishing Company.

Stengel, Richard. (1988, October 24). *Time,* p. 20.

Stengel, Richard, and others. (1988, November 21). Nine key moments. *Time,* pp. 48–56.

Stivers, Richard. (1982). *Evil in modern myth and ritual.* Athens, Georgia: University of Georgia Press.

Szasz, Thomas. (1974). *Ceremonial chemistry: The ritual persecution of drugs, addicts, and pushers.* Garden City, New York: Anchor Press/Doubleday.

Thompson, Laura. (1945). Logico-aesthetic integration in Hopi culture. *American Anthropologist,* 47, 541–553.

Thompson, Robert Farris. (1973). Yoruba artistic criticism. In Warren D'Azevedo (Ed.), *The traditional artist in African societies* (pp. 19–61). Bloomington, Indiana: Indiana University Press.

Throop, Palmer Allen. (1940). *Criticism of the Crusades: A study of public opinion and crusade propaganda.* Amsterdam, The Netherlands: Swets and Zeitlinger.

Tonnies, Ferdinand. (1940). *Fundamental concepts of sociology.* New York: American Book Company.

_____. (1957). *Community and society.* East Lansing: Michigan State University Press.

Tuchman, Gaye. (1978). *Making news: A study in the construction of reality.* New York: Free Press.

Turner, Victor.(1969). *The ritual process.* Chicago: Aldine.

_____. (1986). *The anthropology of performance.* New York: PAJ Publications.

U.S. Department of Commerce, Bureau of the Census. (1990). *Statistical abstracts of the United States, 1990.* Washington, D.C.: U.S. Government Printing Office.

U.S. Congress. (1987). U.S. Congressional Budget Office report for 1987. Washington, D.C.: U.S. Government Printing Office.

Weber, Max. (1947). Theory of social and economic organization. In A.R. Henderson & Talcott Parsons (Trans. and Eds.), *Wirtschaft und Gesellschamd,* Part I (pp. 358–373; 385–392). New York: Oxford University Press.

_____. (1958). *The Protestant ethic and the spirit of capitalism.* New York: Scribner.

_____. (1968). *On charisma and institution building : Selected papers.* Chicago: University of Chicago Press.

Webster's Third International Dictonary of the English Language. (1986). Springfield, Massachusetts: Merriam-Webster.

White, Robert A. (1987). Television as myth and ritual. *Communication Research Trends,* 8(1).

Williams, Raymond. (1975). *Television, technology, and cultural form.* New York: Schocken Books.

Wills, Garry. (1988, November 21). The power populist. *Time,* pp. 61–72.

Appendix A

Political Perception Survey Form

University of Washington
School of Communications

By filling out this questionnaire, you can help our research group analyze the role played by the mass media during the 1988 presidential election. There are three pages to complete. You do not need to write your name on this questionnaire. Thank you for your time!

1) Age on your last birthday _____

2) _____Male   _____Female

3) Year in School: _____Freshman _____Sophomore
                   _____Junior _____Senior _____Graduate

4) Major or intended major: _____

5) In what class are you filling out this survey?
   _____

6) Did you vote in the 1988 presidential election? _____Yes   _____No
                                                   _____Not eligible

7) If Yes, for whom did you vote? _____ Bush _____ Dukakis

8) Would you say that your parent(s) usually vote:
   _____Democrat _____Republican _____Not by party _____Don't know

9) During the months leading up to the election did you talk much about the campaign?

   With your family?_____not at all_____a little _____
                    quite a bit_____ a lot _____

   With your friends_____not at all_____a little_____
                    quite a bit_____ a lot _____

In your classes:_____not at all_____a little_____
                          quite a bit_____   a lot _____

10) How interested in politics are you on a scale of 0 to 10?
(Circle one number.)

   0___1___2___3___4___5___6___7___8___9___10
   not at all interested   very interested

11) Which of the following events did you:
(Check as many as apply for each event).

	watch live on TV	see TV news	read about/hear about highlights
Democratic Convention	☐	☐	☐
Republican Convention	☐	☐	☐
1st Debate: Bush/Dukakis	☐	☐	☐
2nd Debate: Bush/Dukakis	☐	☐	☐
Bentsen/ Quayle Debate	☐	☐	☐
Election Returns	☐	☐	☐

12) What do you remember as the three main issues of the election campaign?

   1. _____

   2. _____

   3. _____

13) If you were the U.S. President and could solve just one problem facing the country today, what problem would you choose?

   _____

14) Please indicate (with a check mark) which characteristics you feel are important for a U.S. president to have. Choose as many as you like.

_____tough	_____good-looking
_____a "Washington insider"	_____experienced in foreign policy
_____tall	_____flexible
_____competent	_____athletic
_____young	_____inspirational
_____honest	_____good with money matters
_____kind	_____realistic
_____a good communicator	_____family-oriented
_____firm religious beliefs	_____a good negotiator
_____knowledgeable about history	_____optimistic
_____male	_____open to new ideas

15) Now using the words from the above list complete the following sentence:

It is most important that our President be:
1)_____
2)_____ and
3)_____
Is there any other word you want to add? _____

16) Which, if any, political advertisements do you remember best from the presidential campaign? (Describe briefly.)

17) Please put a "B" for Bush and a "D" for Dukakis next to any words that you feel describe either one of them. Put both a "B" and "D" next to any words you feel describe them both. Please print the letters clearly.

_____trustworthy	_____intellectual	_____patriotic
_____calculating	_____hard-headed	_____competent
_____honest	_____strong	_____vigorous
_____conservative	_____silk-stocking	_____shrewd
_____privileged	_____realistic	_____nice
_____well-organized	_____liberal	_____boring
_____arrogant	_____all-American	_____presidential

18) Put a check next to the candidate(s) who served in the military.
_____Lloyd Bentsen _____Michael Dukakis
_____George Bush _____Dan Quayle

19) Willie Horton was: (Choose one).

_____On Dukakis' campaign staff
_____In Bush's campaign ads
_____An early Democratic primary contender

20) Please indicate by writing an "L" or a "C" next to the word(s) any of the following you would associate with being "Liberal" or "Conservative." Choose as many or as few as you wish. Please print the letters clearly.

_____using credit	_____personal freedom	_____open minded
_____intellectual	_____traditional	_____patriotic
_____elite	_____free speech	_____reactionary
_____strong legal system	_____progressive	_____competitive markets
_____mainstream	_____family values	_____strong defense

Check the correct answer:

21) The number of young people who can afford to buy their own homes has, since 1978:

____doubled   ____been cut in half   ____stayed about the same

22) The percentage of American households in which both biological parents, married (to each other), live with their children with the father as the main support is about:

_____70–80%   _____10–20%   _____50–60%

23) In a worldwide comparison U.S. public schools (grades K–12) rank #1 worldwide.

_____True_____False

24) If we were going to make a film about the 1988 campaign, which movie star would you pick to play George Bush?

_____

25) Whom would you pick to play the role of Michael Dukakis?

_____

We'd like to talk to you some more about the 1988 campaign. If you're willing to be interviewed sometime in the next week or so, either by telephone or in person, please write down your name, telephone number(s), and day and time where you can be reached and we'll contact you shortly. Thank you for your help!

_____YES, I'm willing to be interviewed:

Name:_____

Day phone:_____Eve:_____

Good time to reach me:_____

(This survey instrument was conceived and designed as part of a University of Washington class project under the direction of Dr. Gladys Engel Lang.)

Appendix B

Respondent Political Profile Form

Spring 1990

Respondent number (assigned) _____
Phone number _____
Sex _____
Age _____
Highest level of education completed _____
Parents' occupations: (mother) _____
                              (father) _____
Estimated annual income of respondent_____
Race (optional)_____
Religion (optional)_____
Sexual Preference (optional)_____

1. How would you describe yourself politically? (Circle one.)

   Conservative   Moderate   Liberal

2. In what political party, if any, are you now registered or affiliated with?

3. If you are not now registered in a political party, in which party were you last registered?

4. Have you ever voted for a candidate who did not belong to the political party in which you are now or have been previously registered or affiliated with?

   ____ Yes   ___ No   ___ Can't recall

5. What percent of the time, do you think, have you voted for some one who was not a member of "your" political party?

    ___ a.) less than 10%
    ___ b.) 10%–30%
    ___ c.) 30%–60%
    ___ d.) 60% or more.

6. For whom did you vote in the last two (1988 and 1984) presidential elections?

    1988 _____
    1984 _____

7. On a scale of one to five, with one representing "least interested" and five representing "very interested," how would you rate your interest in politics? (Circle one number only.)

    1   2   3   4   5

Please indicate days and blocks of time which would best suit your schedule if you continue to participate in this research project. Return forms as soon as possible to Kerric Harvey, Mail Stop DS-40, School of Communications, The University of Washington, Seattle, WA 98195. THANK YOU!

Appendix C

Research Instrument for Panel Analysis of Mythic Themes in Pre-election Night Television Advertisements

---

Spring 1990

Respondent number   Date of analysis

PART I. Unstructured Analysis:

Please watch the following two videotapes carefully. Watch one tape first and then the other, following the directions given to you verbally by the researcher. On the appropriate logging form for each video, please jot down your impressions from the tape you just watched, regarding a.) the candidates; b.) the campaign issues, and; c.) the United States in general. (You may wish to divide your paper into three columns headed "candidate," "issues," "nation" to help you organize your comments.) Please explain your answers by referring back to specific things within each tape. Write in whatever style feels the most comfortable; you do not have to write in complete sentences. Please feel free to pause the tape if you need more time to get your observations down on paper.

Once you're done with this part of the analysis, please take a few moments to collect your thoughts before proceeding to Parts II and III. DO NOT DISCUSS YOUR ANSWERS WITH ANY ONE DURING THIS TIME.

PART II. Structured Analysis

Please indicate which of the following values or beliefs you feel are mentioned during the videotape that you just watched by checking them off on the lists below. Leave blank those items which you feel were not mentioned at all. Once you finish Part II, please go directly to Part III and repeat the checking-off process for that list as well.

____ 1. All men are created equal.
____ 2. People have a right to be happy.
____ 3. God is a higher power than earthly government.
____ 4. Personal liberty is the most important human freedom.
____ 5. Government is answerable to the people.
____ 6. People should have a "say" in making laws that affect them.
____ 7. The state should protect freedom of religion.
____ 8. We are all in this together.
____ 9. All true patriots wish to serve their country.
____ 10. Innocent until proven guilty.
____ 11. People have a right to privacy.
____ 12. Hard work and honesty will make you rich.
____ 13. America is the guardian of world democracy.
____ 14. Democracy is the best form of government for every one.
____ 15. The law treats everyone fairly and equally.
____ 16. The rights of the many outweigh the rights of the few.
____ 17. Given the facts and freedom to debate them, people will make the most
        reasonable decision.
____ 18. Opportunity only knocks once.
____ 19. You get what you pay for.
____ 20. Everything has its price.
____ 21. God is on the side of the right and just.
____ 22. Progress is a wonderful thing.
____ 23. Violence is justified by self-defense.
____ 24. Winner take all.
____ 25. More is better.
____ 26. There are no problems we cannot solve.
____ 27. Where there's a will, there's a way.
____ 28. People get what they deserve.
____ 30. If you work hard enough, you'll succeed.
____ 31. It's not whether you win or lose; it's how you play the game.
____ 32. Peace through strength.
____ 33. Drugs are America's number one problem.
____ 34. America is a land of endless opportunity.
____ 35. Things just keep getting better.
____ 36. Less government is better government.
____ 37. America is #1.
____ 38. People are basically good.
____ 39. The strong must protect the weak.
____ 40. Survival of the fittest is the best rule of business.

PART III. Leadership Styles

In this final section, please think back to the tape you have just watched and indicate with a checkmark those items on the following two lists that you feel each candidate displayed or claimed to possess during the course of his advertisement. Check as many items as you feel apply to each man. Leave blank any items which you feel do not apply.

_____

Candidate name

During the course of this videotape, the candidate came across as:
(type of leader)

___ 41. a champion
___ 42. a defender of the weak
___ 43. a man of the people
___ 44. a crusader for human rights
___ 45. a martyr
___ 46. a spiritual leader
___ 47. a golden boy
___ 48. a smooth operator/sharp dresser
___ 49. a man destined to be president
___ 50. a self-made man
___ 51. a tough guy
___ 52. a philosopher
___ 53. a family man
___ 54. a father figure
___ 55. a patriarch
___ 56. a bully
___ 57. a loner
___ 58. a team player
___ 59. a warrior

The candidate also portrayed himself as being:
___ 60. self-reliant
___ 61. honest
___ 62. a good communicator
___ 63. realistic
___ 64. open to new ideas
___ 65. kind/sensitive
___ 66. good-looking

___ 67. all-American
___ 68. a good negotiator
___ 69. patriotic
___ 70. competent
___ 71. tall
___ 72. stable
___ 73. decisive
___ 74. larger than life

Now, please choose three items from any of the lists contained anywhere on this form and list them in the order in which you feel they were emphasized during the course of the videotape you just watched. They may be items about the candidate, about the issues, or about the world and the United States in general.

75. _____

76. _____

77. _____

If you were a movie producer making a film biography of each candidate, what actor would you select to play the role of:

78. George Bush: _____

79. Michael Dukakis: _____

80. Were there any specific impressions you received from this tape that we did not list anywhere on this form?

THANK YOU FOR YOUR PARTICIPATION IN THIS PROJECT. WITHOUT YOUR HELP, IT COULD NOT HAVE HAPPENED.